PAULA TROPE
EMANCIPATORY ACTION

Published in conjunction with the exhibition *Emancipatory Action: Paula Trope and the Meninos*, presented at the Americas Society Art Gallery from May 24 to August 31, 2007.

Emancipatory Action: Paula Trope and the Meninos was organized with the David Rockefeller Center for Latin American Studies. The exhibition was made possible with public funds from the New York State Council on the Arts, a State Agency; by the generous support of The Jacques and Natasha Gelman Trust; and by Humberto and Claudia Carvalho.

Funds for the catalogue have been provided by the Bruce T. Halle Family Foundation. The exhibition was the Visual Arts component of the Americas Society's "Embrace Brazil" festival. Funding for this series was provided by David Rockefeller.

Cover:
Paula Trope in collaboration with Muller
Front: *Untitled (Money)*
Back: *Muller, 8 years old, watcher of cars*
From the series *Os Meninos* (*The Boys*), 1993–94
Pinhole camera photography
Collection of the artist, Rio de Janeiro

Editor
Gabriela Rangel

Editorial Assistant
Isabela Villanueva

Editorial Intern
Alessandra Caputo

Translations
Erin Goodman (Portuguese)
Christopher Winks (Spanish)

Transcription of Sevcenko-Trope Interview
Gabriel Rocha

Roundtable Transcription
Kathryn Moioli

Copyeditor
Marcie Muscat

Design
Elvira Morán / elviradesigns.com

Published by the Americas Society
680 Park Avenue, New York, NY 10021

Printed in West Haven, Conn., USA, by GHP

PAULA TROPE
EMANCIPATORY ACTION

AMERICAS SOCIETY

TABLE OF CONTENTS

ACKNOWLEDGMENTS
SUSAN SEGAL

The Americas Society was delighted to present *Emancipatory Action: Paula Trope and the Meninos*, the first exhibition in the United States dedicated to these pioneering works of Brazilian photography and video art. Trope is one of Brazil's most original artistic voices, and along with the exhibition, the present publication offers a survey of her work, which proposes a profound examination of issues related to authorship and artistic collaboration vis-à-vis critical tensions between the ethics and aesthetics that have permeated the last decades of Brazilian art, as well as contemporary art practices elsewhere.

Paula Trope defines herself artistically as a mediator within a complex process of symbolic exchanges with the subjects/coauthors of her works, whom she meets in the streets of Rio de Janeiro. She begins this process by making pinhole cameras from tin cans and then distributing them to the subjects of her portraits, the *meninos* (children and adolescents living on the streets or in the favelas), thus empowering them to collaborate in crafting their own images.

Emancipatory Action: Paula Trope and the Meninos included works from the series *Os Meninos* (*The Boys*), which comprises diptychs formed by Trope's pictures of the children alongside the pictures taken by those portrayed. In the subsequent award-winning series *Sem Simpatia* (*Without Sympathy*), Trope photographed *meninos* in front of an urban-planning project in Rio de Janeiro wherein each teenager was asked to reinvent in maquettes the favelas of Rio de Janeiro and then depict his "recreation" of the city and its daily life. The exhibition also featured the series *Contos de Passagem* (*Passage Tales*), in which Trope captured through pinhole video the relationships she established with the street children; and the series *Traslados* (*On the Move*), in which she promoted interchanges between Cuban and Brazilian children in a slide installation created for the Sixth Havana Biennial in 1997.

For more than forty years, the Americas Society has exposed audiences in the United States to the arts and cultures of their neighbors in the Western Hemisphere. *Emancipatory Action: Paula Trope and the Meninos* continues this pioneering tradition. Americas Society has held several notable shows on Brazilian art, but this was the first to address the country's socially engaged art.

This exhibition was made possible by the efforts of many individuals and institutions. We wish to first thank Paula Trope, who has been instrumental in all phases of planning the exhibition, for her professionalism and dedication. Americas Society was fortunate to entrust the curatorship of this exhibition to Gabriela Rangel, Director of our Visual Arts Department, with the collaboration of José Luis Falconi, curator of Latin American and Latino Art at the David Rockefeller Center for Latin American Studies at Harvard University. I would like to acknowledge their extraordinary dedication to this project.

In Brazil, we acknowledge the Coleção Gilberto Chateaubriand of the Museu de Arte Moderna in Rio de Janeiro for lending their works and for their ongoing support. We are also grateful to the Galeria Vermelho in São Paulo, and in particular to Marcus Gallon for his advice and expertise. Thanks are also due to Paulo Roberto Santi, who so kindly lent artworks to this exhibition; we are also grateful to him for initiating contact with Paula Trope.

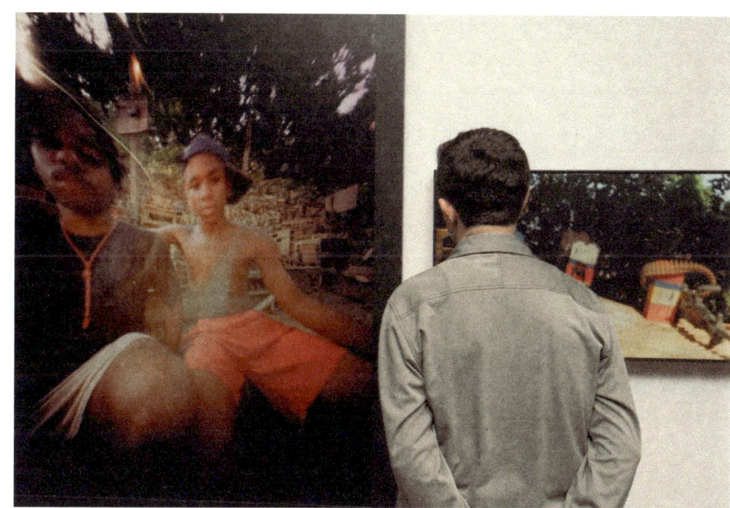

Installation view of *Emancipatory Action: Paula Trope and the Meninos*
at the Americas Society Art Gallery, 2007
Photograph by Arturo Sánchez

We would like to extend our deepest appreciation to Ute Meta Bauer, Carrie Lambert-Beatty, Linda Norden, Lane Relyea, Nicolau Sevcenko, and Doris Sommer for participating in a roundtable discussion on relational aesthetics and participatory art at Harvard University in April 2007, a transcription of which is included in this publication. Americas Society would especially like to acknowledge the generous financial support of the New York State Council on the Arts, a State Agency; The Jacques and Natasha Gelman Trust; and Humberto and Claudia Carvalho. We are most grateful to the Bruce T. Halle Family Foundation for funding this publication.

This exhibition was the Visual Arts component of the Embrace Brazil festival, which explored the modern and contemporary art, literature, and music of this giant among South American nations. This festival could not have been realized without the very generous support of David Rockefeller.

The Americas Society is very fortunate to have an extremely dedicated Visual Arts staff. We are most thankful for the hard work of Gabriela Rangel, Director of Visual Arts and Curator of the Art Gallery; Isabela Villanueva, Assistant Curator; Marcia Cohen and Mariela Hardy, the former and current Exhibitions and Public Programs Coordinators; and Alessadra Caputo, Editorial Intern. We would like to express our gratitude to our hard-working art handlers Eric Lu, Ferrán Martin, Ian Pedigo, and Arturo Sánchez. We are also most appreciative to Andrea Sanseverino Galan, Senior Director of Foundation and Institutional Giving.

The realization of this exhibition greatly benefited from the advice and support offered so generously by Paulo Herkenhoff and the other members of the Americas Society Visual Arts Advisory Board. We record here our special thanks to them.

PAULA TROPE: BETWEEN SHIRT AND SKIN
GABRIELA RANGEL

If, in making a portrait, you hope to grasp the interior silence of a willing victim, it's very difficult, but you must somehow position the camera between the shirt and the skin.
—Henri Cartier-Bresson

How can one represent subjects who have been deprived of visibility with something that is itself produced fragmentarily and from a position of invisibility? This difficult question, implicit in the blurred portraits of children and young people by the artist Paula Trope, is echoed by the oxymoronic concept of "seeing with our blind gaze." Indeed, Trope's large-format color photographs, made in different moments and modes of collaboration with her subjects, revisit problems that have been examined by traditional cinematic realism in which the filmmaker is posited as a witness or observer, challenged with the task of disembodying his or her style to bring the image into an ontology of the authentic wherein that which is shown and that which is seen are transcriptions of the real. By refusing to "transcribe" reality on the basis of the identity conferred by the portrait, Trope takes up a debate developed within Neorealism, which altered the mechanical quality of realistic action to bring about an "increase in purely optical situations."[1] Gilles Deleuze contends that Neorealism's true contribution, beyond the social content of its plotlines, lay in its particular aesthetic approach and in its development of a "new form of reality, supposedly dispersive, elliptical, wandering, or oscillating, which operates through blocs and with deliberately weak nexuses and floating events."[2] Also, Trope's portraits, rife as they are with "weak nexuses" and "floating events," invite a rethinking of the debates proposed by the artist Hélio Oiticica, who posited that poverty is a zone of invisibility, or the indissoluble obverse of the processes of modernity and modernization in the periphery.

I propose to examine certain aspects of Trope's work in relation to the myriad issues and concerns raised by Brazilian film and visual arts in the 1950s and 1960s. Serving as a significant counterpoint to this debate is *Camera Lucida,* Alfredo Jaar's series of photographs of the Catia neighborhood in Caracas, Venezuela. While Trope is not specifically connected to this project, Jaar's method of collaboration with the Catia community presents an exceptional case within the repertory of images that characterize the representations of marginality in contemporary art and photography. Therefore, *Camera Lucida* provides a useful framework for analyzing the procedures proposed by Trope's work in terms of the artistic practices that today provide models for collaboration between artists and marginalized subjects.

CINEMA NOVO, NEOCONCRETISM, AND THE OPTICAL DRAMA OF THE OPPRESSED

For nearly two decades, Paula Trope has assembled a body of photographic work within a framework of collaboration with young people, most of them minors who live on the streets and adolescent residents of the Morro do Pereirão favela in Rio de Janeiro.[3] The tension issuing from Trope's imprecise images retrospectively proposes an approach to the problem of otherness within the technical-practical framework offered by the film and visual arts of 1960s Brazil.

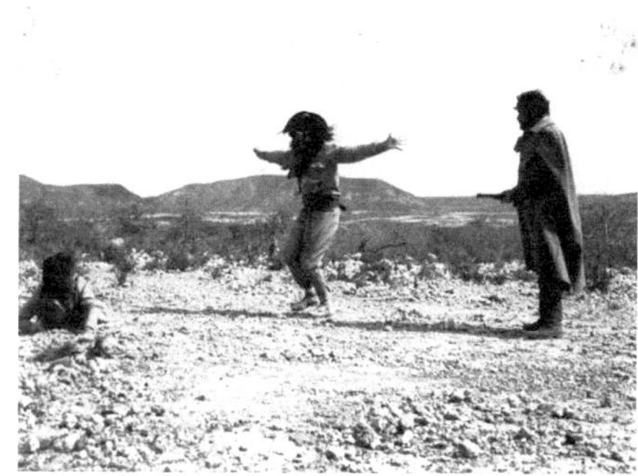

Glauber Rocha, *Deus e o Diabo na Terra do Sol*, 1964
Image courtesy of Acervo Tempo Glauber, Rio de Janeiro

Trained in film theory, Trope examines the invisibility of modernity's "other" side to position photography—and specifically portraiture—as a critical and participatory social practice. By developing blurred portraits of children and youths who, because of their position in society, have been excluded from the process of modernization, Trope displays the contradictions that defined that very process in Brazil, whose logic historically has been marked by drastic social, economic, and political changes driven by developmentalism. In so doing, Trope proposes, on the one hand, to question photography's (or film's) technological determinism, founded in the progress of the optical and chemical device, and, on the other hand, to adopt a non-indexical approach to the portrait through a participatory interchange with subjects who have been erased from that process.[4] In this regard, it is worth noting that the rapid economic growth of this South American country was accompanied by a dizzying demographic explosion in its cities and, consequently, the emergence of profound social disparities, the strengthening of a powerful industrial class, and the blossoming of a vigorous workers' movement. However, this period, which led to a military dictatorship, endured in the international imagination through the elegant melodies of Bossa Nova and the extraordinary voluntarism that culminated in the construction of the city of Brasilia.[5] Paradoxically, this period also witnessed the appearance of favelas, informal shantytowns built by the multitudes of rural citizens who moved into the city and who took to occupying vacant plots in the metropolis in the effort to improve their living conditions.[6]

The genealogy of Trope's antirealistic style of portraiture can be traced back to the production strategies and stylistic methods of Cinema Novo. Emerging after the formation of the Neoconcrete art groups Frente and Ruptura, Cinema Novo was founded at the end of the 1950s by Glauber Rocha and a group of Brazilian filmmakers as a political platform whose aims were not limited to merely opening a cultural space for the country's experimental cinema, but to liberating that space from the ideological domination of the North American culture industry.[7] Rocha and the members of the Cinema Novo proposed a visual revolution whose goal was to operate in the material conditions of underdevelopment. The vertiginous appearance and development of this movement; the international uproar provoked by its aesthetic-political postulates, which articulated a peripheral discourse; and the virulence of its mythic images of peasants, landowners, and bandits from the northeast preceded the installation of the military dictatorship.[8]

Alongside its links to Cinema Novo, Trope's work exhibits an alignment with that of Hélio Oiticica, who based his artistic production on his experiences in the Mangueira favela. At the beginning of the 1960s, by confronting his

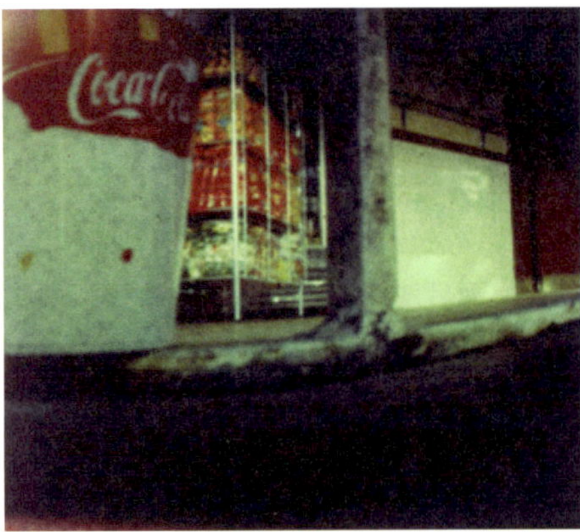

Paula Trope in collaboration with
Desidírio, Janderson, and Fabrício,
Sem título (O Copo do McDonald),
(*Untitled [McDonald's Glass]*)

From the series *Os Meninos* (*The Boys*), 1993–94
Pinhole camera photography on colored resin paper
Collection of the artist, Rio de Janeiro

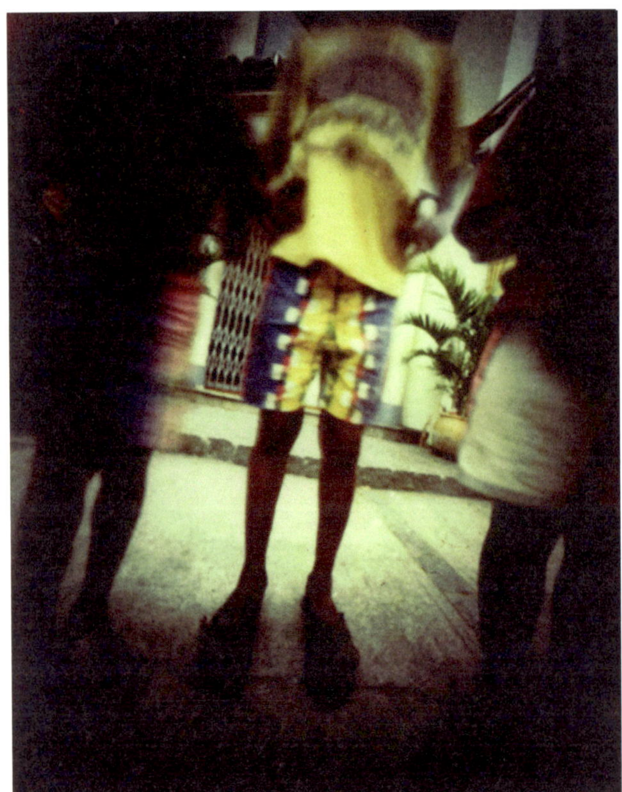

Paula Trope in collaboration with Desidírio, Janderson, and Fabrício,
Desidírio, Janderson, e Fabrício

From the series *Os Meninos* (*The Boys*), 1993–94
Pinhole camera photography on colored resin paper
Collection of the artist, Rio de Janeiro

autonomous field of endeavor with the endemic problems of poverty and underdevelopment, Oiticica began to address social problems consonant with the ethical possibilities of experimental art in Brazil. He developed a close relationship with the samba community of the Mangueira favela, where he worked out his ideas: "The discovery of the *parangolé* elements in the landscape of the urban rural world is also part of establishing perceptive-structural relations between what grows in the structural grid of the *parangolé* (representing here the general character of colour-structure in environmental space) and what is found in the spatial-environmental world. In the architecture of the favela, for example, there is implicitly a *parangolé* character."[9] This process led to a radical questioning of traditional artistic media, which the artist deepened through a study of the reception of the neo-avant-garde readymade. During these years of searching for alternative languages in painting and sculpture, which would ultimately enable his adapting of an experimental artistic practice to underdeveloped conditions of production, Oiticica joined the Mangueira samba school, where he conceived his first *parangolés,* or participatory paintings, made to be worn on the body. In this way he began a critical revision of his own work, unleashing a radical process that, according to Guy Brett, led him to sail in almost all the seas of recent art, exploring topics that addressed "the status of the object as communication or consumer commodity; notions of authorship and the relation of the artist to the audience; the gap between fine art and popular culture; questions of identity, sexuality, colonization, and cultural difference; the relationship between art and life."[10]

Both Rocha and Oiticica posited unconventional practices wherein both the vernacular and the popular understanding of the imaginary adopted epic forms of expression. Oiticica, a defender of the oppressed's right to individual insurrection, identified the anthropological breach separating experimental art from society, and power as an ethical moment, in a visual poem that marked an accentual point in his work. This work, *Bólide Caixa 18, Poema Caixa 2, Homenagem à Cara de Cavalo*, was dedicated to a thief who was shot by the police and whose death, according to Oiticica, showed how "violence is justified as a means of revolt but never as an oppressive one." Through it, the artist broached the difficulties involved in moving beyond individual forms of rebellion to the revolution of a collective social body, a so-called turn of the screw that Rocha, for his part, proposed through the concept of hunger. For Rocha, hunger was an entity that generated a spirit of resistance and insurrection favorable to the violence necessary to enact historical change. According to Ismail Xavier, what was "noteworthy in Rocha was the sense of geopolitics (of which film is one of two vectors) as a fact of a confrontation in which the oppressed can only become visible (and an eventual subject of the process) through violence."[11]

THE FAVELA AS IMAGINED COMMUNITY

When considering the process of "invisible visualization" that is proposed by Trope's blurred portraits in relation to the dominant perceptions of marginality in the visual arts of 1960s Brazil, it is appropriate to situate her work within the sphere of an imagined national community, which, according to Beatriz Jaguaribe, is represented in the present by the favela. For Jaguaribe, "the locus of the 'national imagined community' [is] a 'fearful stain' on the landscape of modernity."[12] This dual vision of the shantytown of misery not only represents the fissures of modernity in Brazil but has also been transformed into a dominant, stereotypical image in which the locus of economic and social deprivation has come to be seen as an illusory symbol that harbors a creative community, where samba, funk, and the colors of Carnival vibrate in such a way as to operate along with its dialectical opposite. The representation of the favela would today be inextricably linked to a social threat, embodied in the autonomous and impenetrable shantytown, besieged by the violence of criminal gangs, prostitution, illegal businesses, and the consumption and distribution of drugs.

Within this framework, Jaguaribe has examined the application of various realist narrative models in the televisual representation of marginality, even as she recognizes that "not all the representations of the favela rely on a realist register, but those that have had greater repercussions and press coverage have made use of the impact of verisimilitude associated with the realistic encoding of the real."[13] These models, bearers of the "shock of the real" by means of an "artistic defamiliarization," were developed on the basis of literary and cinematic narratives related to the construction of a discourse of modernity in Brazil. In this regard, Trope's work operates at cross-purposes to realism as a formula for representing the conditions of exclusion that have accompanied modernization, exploring the need to reverse the effects of defamiliarization that are the result of the violent images that represent the favela.

As suggested by Jaguaribe, the motto *"seja marginal, seja héroi"* (printed on a flag conceived by Oiticica at the end of the 1960s and consequently banned by the dictatorship) and the *bólide*-poem dedicated to the thief Cara de Cavalo are ideas that have, in the present, been instrumentalized to romanticize the status of favela dwellers.[14] This practice of defamiliarization reinforces the exclusionary system questioned by Oiticica in his time, a normalized interpretation of which is today deconstructed by

means of a purely visual discourse in Trope's nebulous photographs. I am referring to the search for an optical mechanism that can suspend the defamiliarization produced by realist representations of the Brazilian favelas, particularly those used in fictional works with broad public impact, such as the popular *telenovelas* broadcast by Rede Globo and the films *Pixote* (1981), by Héctor Babenco, and *Cidade de Deus* (2002), by Katia Lund and Fernando Meirelles (the latter based on Paulo Lins's 1997 novel of the same name). It was Miguel Rio Branco, a member of the prestigious Magnum photo agency and clearly a point of reference for Trope, who paradoxically pioneered this kind of antirealist approach to the documentary image in Brazil through the use of chiaroscuro and chromatic expressionism. The influence of cinema verité on the nonlinear treatment of documentary impelled Rio Branco to break with the conventions of photojournalism in his approach to prostitutes, youths, and children living in popular neighborhoods of Rio de Janeiro, showing the individuals consciously posing for the camera, and using color in an allegorical fashion.

Trope's refusal to identify the impoverished landscape of the favela and clearly depict the faces of its inhabitants complicates the indexical relationship between subject and context. To do this, she avails herself of precinematographic procedures through the use of optico-mechanical artifacts, which she fabricates with recycled cookie canisters and expired film stock. A digression may be necessary to understand this methodology: the favela as we know it in its present-day, realist codification took almost two decades to become part of the repertory of Brazilian film and television.[15] *Rio 40 Graus*, a pioneering film shot by Nelson Pereira dos Santos in a Rio de Janeiro favela in 1955, served as a catalyst for the

Cinema Novo generation, inspiring them to make aesthetically ambitious and thematically committed films with the aim of creating an independent auteurist cinema.[16] Pereira dos Santos's film, made according to Neorealist precepts, was censored by the police shortly after its premiere, hindering its distribution. Nonetheless, this film opened a critical discussion on the realist model, enabling its aesthetic reconsideration in the context of the modernization of an underdeveloped country and revealing the social contradictions inherent in Brazil's economic expansion—a subject that would later be addressed by Rocha in films that took a direction opposed to that of Pereira dos Santos.

Reflecting on photography's role as a social mediator, Trope has declared that her practice is a response to the values that Brecht attributed to gesture and attitude: "Photography, in a certain way, is much closer to theater (a specific concept of theater) than to the social exercise of photography as is generally thought."[17] Trope has organized encounters with her subjects in various situations and places within the urban fabric of Rio de Janeiro and other cities, both sporadically and more consistently over time, which in turn determines the type and extent of collaboration with her subjects. On a primary level, the pact established between the artist and her subjects entails the making of individual or group portraits, with the aim of drawing participants into the construction of their own images, and on any subject whatsoever.

In the series *Os Meninos* (1993–94), large-format diptychs made with street children in Rio de Janeiro, Trope first established a connection with her subjects before photographing them in their neighborhoods of Ipanema, Leblon, Copacabana, and Barra da Tijuca. She observed the children's inter-actions with police, shopkeepers, and citizens in these affluent or recently gentrified districts, plotting the trajectories that took shape as the children sought out informal labor in order to survive, as well as the dangers they faced living in such extreme conditions. The first diptych in the series shows an image of an unfolded 100-cruzeiro banknote alongside a portrait of an eight-year-old boy named Muller, who chose to accompany his photo with the bill as proof of his earnings from watching parked cars.

On the one hand, the gazes of those portrayed in *Os Meninos* are aimed directly at the camera, acknowledging the existence of the optical-registering equipment. However, the imprecision of the images deliberately separates them from traditional modes of representing poverty, whose repertory of images is internationally disseminated via news agencies and photojournalists and broadcast on a mass level in Brazil's successful television productions. *Os Meninos* reverses the economy of these representations—which privilege the context and physiognomy of subjects who have been excluded from or deprived of the basic conditions of life— and substitutes it with what Deleuze describes as an "optical drama."[18] The series proposes a type of opaque narrative that omits presence in favor of the imaginary gaze, one that transforms the real into the imaginary but that, at the same time, produces a *new* reality. If every image obtained by the artist is accompanied by one or several counter-images captured by one or several collaborators, then what might have been straightforward representations of marginalized children within an urban or semiurban context become instead imprecise, distorted portraits accompanied by varied images: a grille protecting a storefront, an oversized banknote, the eaves of a building—images that dismantle the catalogue of distinctions between real and imaginary, past and present, life and death.

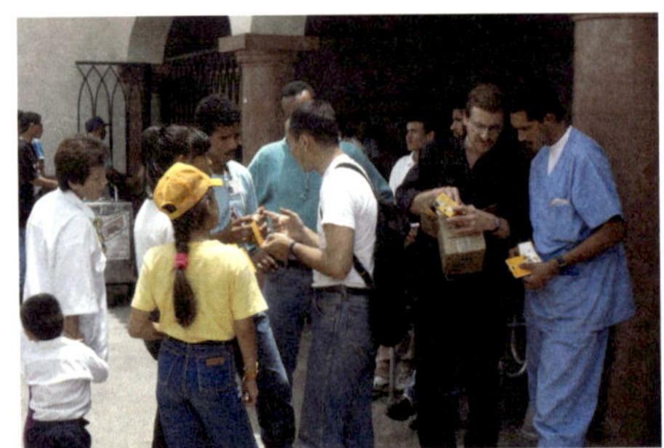

Alfredo Jaar distributiong cameras to the people who collaborated in *Camera Lucida*, 1996
Image courtesy of the artist

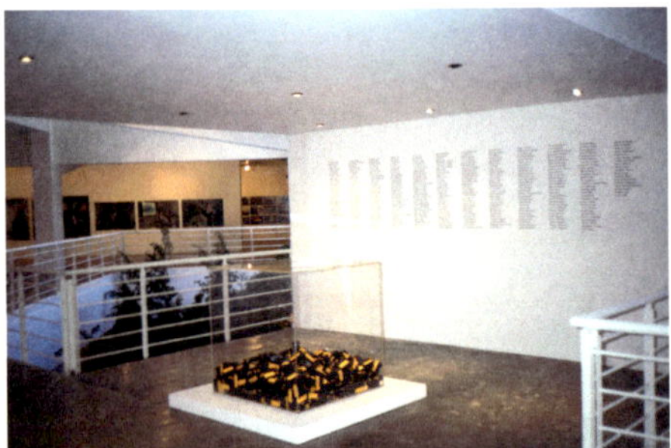

Installation view of Alfredo Jaar's *Camera Lucida* at the exhibition *Cuarta Pared*, Museo Jacobo Borges, Caracas, 1996
Images courtesy of the artist

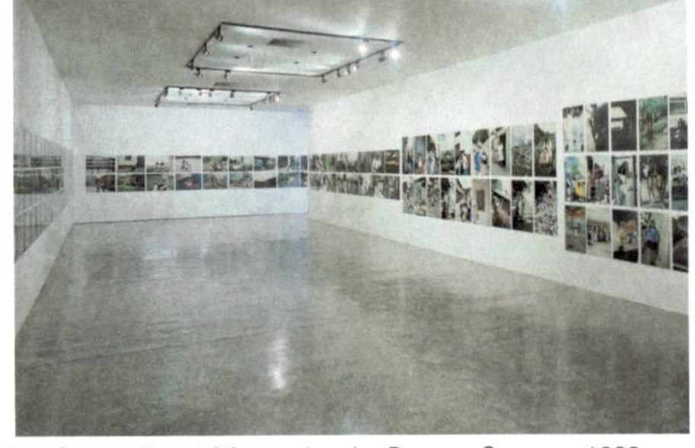

On another level, Trope takes into consideration Guy Debord's critique of the culture industry to show that, in the society of the spectacle, the excess of images has transformed the real into a simulacrum: "The relationships between people are mediated by images, an abstraction of the real, and the subject hidden behind that discourse, dematerialized, is the social mechanism itself."[19] Along with the large format used in the series *Os Meninos* and *Sem Simpatia,* the distortion produced by the curvature of the camera obscura, the life-size enlargement of the negative of the expired film stock, and the laboratory work that extracts high-intensity colors in the high contrast replace action and the causes and effects of poverty with the indeterminacy of the subject's context, breaking down the defamiliarization produced by the systematic repetition of images of violence.

THE ARTIST AS PRODUCER

Trope teaches her collaborators how to use photographic mechanisms made from discarded cans and then includes the images made by her subjects alongside her own. Nonetheless, the artist maintains creative control over the production and presentation of the photographs. Alfredo Jaar used analogous procedures in his project *Camera Lucida* (1996), whose date of realization coincides with Trope's *Os Meninos.*

In response to an invitation to participate in a group show that would inaugurate the recently opened Museo Jacobo Borges in Caracas, Jaar devised a project through which both he and the museum could establish a direct relationship with the working-class district where the institution was located. Jaar distributed 1,000 disposable Kodacolor cameras to 1,000 residents of Catia, one of the most densely populated areas of Caracas with a high degree of poverty and urban violence. The invitation to participate was sent exclusively to the residents of Catia and endorsed by the museum through grassroots organizations like the Ateneo de Catia, which is dedicated to the promotion of community culture, and community centers whose mission is to address social problems affecting youth.

Jaar's texts proposed the following rules:
You are invited to use this camera with complete freedom.
You have ten days in which to do so.
After taking the twelve (12) photos this camera contains, bring it all to the Ateneo de Catia. . . .
Request a number you can use to stop by the Ateneo de Catia a week later to claim the photos you took, completely free of charge. You will be asked to choose one for exhibition in the new Museo Jacobo Borges, opening soon.[20]

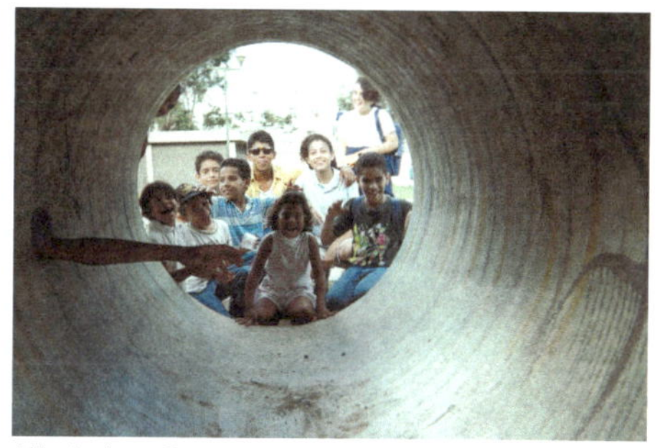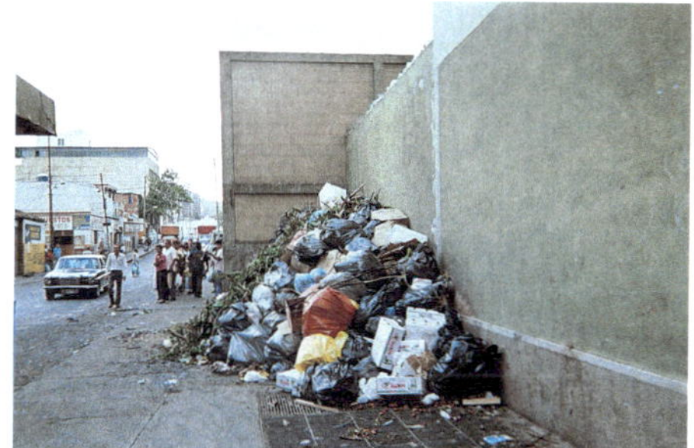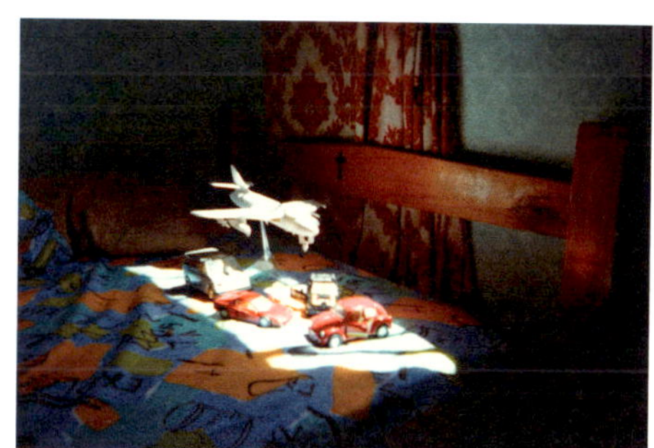

Alfredo Jaar, *Camera Lucida*, 1996
Images courtesy of the artist

Camera Lucida was made expressly for the group show *Cuarta Pared* (*Fourth Wall*), an exhibition of photographs taken by the recipients of the disposable cameras.[21] Inspired by the book of the same name by the post-structuralist writer Roland Barthes,[22] *Camera Lucida* envisioned the free distribution of these color photographs to the participants once they had followed the steps outlined in the call.

Jaar, working as an artist-producer, organized the images according to conventional categories, assembling them into groups determined by genre—portraits, urban landscapes, domestic scenes, etc. The participants' names were included along with a wall text in which Jaar explained the conceptual bases of the project. In a large acrylic box in the museum gallery, the carcasses of the disposable cameras were exhibited within a mechanism that, by revealing the process through which the images were produced, evoked visual tactics similar to those utilized by the art collective Art & Language. The photographs were distributed in groups according to size: 100 x 150 cm, 50 x 75 cm, 40 x 60 cm, and 20 x 30 cm.

Additionally, the exhibition design proposed by Jaar undermined the hierarchy of the images by arranging them in grids, thus engaging—through the recovery of the utopian and creative potential of photography as a medium within everyone's reach—the supposed ecumenical humanism of historical undertakings such as *The Family of Man*[23] to generate an experience of public art that was specific, community-oriented, and open-ended. The project became even more pertinent upon taking into consideration the public debate in Caracas regarding the (ir)relevance of the Museo Jacobo Borges, whose founding by presidential decree touched off a heated polemic, as it was constructed in a district surrounded by a sprawling shantytown. Moreover, the museum was built on land located within the only recreational park in the neighborhood and next to one of the most repressive, overcrowded prisons in the country.[24] While admission to museums is free in Venezuela, the population to whom Jaar's photographic project was directed rarely visits them. *Camera Lucida* not only invigorated the formerly passive rapport that Catia residents had with an institution far removed from their interests, but also featured images that the community itself had generated within a space reserved for exhibiting aesthetically accomplished works. Through reciprocal participation, Jaar's project mapped the conditions of the place, incorporating the neighborhood's habits, daily life, characters, aspirations, and unresolved problems.

In a similar vein, Trope was one of several artists and filmmakers to be invited to document a project in the favela of Vila Pereira da Silva, better known as the Morro do Pereirão.[25] After spending some time in the community, she produced the series *Sem Simpatia*, which comprises portraits of youths living in the favela.[26] The series includes partial views, selected by her young subjects, of the *Proyecto Morrinho*, an extraordinary oversize model of the shantytown, which they had built on a vacant lot. Because of violence caused by drug trafficking, illegal businesses, mafia-related conflict, and police corruption, adolescents could not freely enjoy Morro do Pereirão's public spaces, so, using discarded materials, this group of young people constructed a replica of their community on a corner of the lot. What began as a game or a spontaneous exercise of creativity and freedom was transformed into an important collective exercise in public art, which eventually involved other young people and gave the entire community of Morro do Pereirão an importance beyond its immediate context. Public opinion in Rio de Janeiro began to shift, and the favela residents became conscious of the democratic potential of this undertaking, which resulted in the reclaiming of a public space that had been besieged by violence. The aspirations of these young people were projected onto a regional and national scale, breaking the confines of a city that previously had offered them no possibility of enjoying even a minimum level of rights.

The series *Sem Simpatia* does not directly document the creation of the model, but it does present individual and group portraits of the participants, presented in triptychs and polyptychs, accompanied by partial views of the model *Morrinho* that were selected by the subjects as representations of their own creative involvement. This series, also created using camera obscuras and expired film stock, took Trope's experimental approach to portraiture to a new and distinct level of commitment: her collaborative method expanded the reach of her authorial limits by appointing the subjects from Morro do Pereirão as coauthors of the photos, and she also offered them an equal share of the profits obtained from the sale of any piece in the series. Its title, which translates literally as "without sympathy" (or, alternatively, "without pity"), is an ironic nuance provided by Trope's subject-collaborators that pronounces the silent but willing voice of the victim, thus allowing the artist to position the camera between the shirt and the skin.

1   Gilles Deleuze, *La imagen-tiempo, estudios sobre cine 2*, trans. Irene Agoff (Buenos Aires: Paidos, 2007), p. 13.

2   Deleuze, *op. cit.* (note 1), p. 11.

3   This body of work has been expanded through the use of obsolete video cameras manipulated by the artist to create distortion in the formation of the image.

4   In the case of Brazil, such transformations were propelled mainly by President Juscelino Kubitschek.

5   The city was designed by the Brazilian architects Lucio Costa and Oscar Niemeyer and inaugurated in 1960.

6   Mário Pedrosa estimated that "during the crucial decade of 1940–1950, in which a kind of industrialization took shape through the mechanism of import substitution, the country's urban population grew 45% with a population increase of 10,500,000, of which 5,800,000 were absorbed by the urban sector. . . . Concomitantly with this brutal uprooting of people into the cities, the working class doubled during this decade." See M. Pedrosa, "A Bienal de cá pra lá," in Aracy Amaral, ed., *Mundo, Homem, Arte em Crise*. 2nd ed. (São Paulo: Perspectiva, 1986), pp. 254–56.

7   The Neoconcrete movement took place in the cities of Rio de Janeiro and São Paulo, spurred on by figures including Oiticica, Ferreira Gullar, Mário Pedrosa, Abraham Palatnik, Ivan Serpa, Lygia Pape, Lygia Clark, Geraldo de Barros, Willys de Castro, Waldemar Cordeiro, and Almir Mavignier, among others. The debate generated by Rocha regarding

the role of national cultural production in the development of modern Brazilian society was on a par with the concerns of the experimental theater and literature of that period.

8   Already in 1961, the film critic and screenwriter Orlando Sena admitted: "Like any revolution, this is one beginning violently, and we are obliged to be violent." Quoted in Alex Viany, "Old and New Brazilian Cinema," *TDR: The Drama Review,* vol. 14, no. 2 (Winter 1970), p. 142.

9   Hélio Oiticica, "Fundamental Bases for the Definition of the Parangolé, November 1964," in *Hélio Oiticica* (Rio de Janeiro: Projeto Hélio Oiticica, 1996), p. 87.

10   Guy Brett, "The Experimental Exercise of Freedom," in *Hélio Oiticica* (Rio de Janeiro: Projeto Hélio Oiticica, 1996), pp. 223–24.

11   Ismail Xavier, "Preface," in *Revolução de Cinema Novo, Glauber Rocha* (São Paulo: Cosac Naify, 2004), p. 21.

12   Beatriz Jaguaribe, "Favelas and the Aesthetics of Realism: Representations in Film and Literature," *Journal of Latin American Studies*, vol. 13 (December 2004), pp. 327–42.

13   Jaguaribe, *op. cit.* (note 12), p. 328.

14   Oiticica repeated the motto in a *parangolé.*

15   Jaguaribe contends that the realist narrative models only gained popularity and mass appeal with the expansion of Brazilian television in the 1970s, that is, during the most aggressive stage of modernization.

16   It is no accident that Pereira dos Santos built a movie camera for the film *Vidas secas* (1963), which enabled him to reflect the material conditions of poverty in northeastern Brazil.

17   Gabriela Rangel, "Paula Trope and the 'Meninos do Morrinho,'" *Review: Literature and Arts of the Americas*, vol. 39, no. 2 (November 2009), p. 278.

18   Deleuze, *op. cit.* (note 1), p. 21.

19   Rangel, *op. cit.* (note 17), p. 279.

20   See *Cuarta Pared* (Catalogue no. 38), exh. cat. (Caracas: Museo Jacobo Borges, 1996), pp. 38–39.

21   *Cuarta Pared* was on view at the Museo Jacobo Borges in Caracas from March 24 to May 25, 1996. It was curated by Jesús Fuenmayor and included works by José Gabriel Fernández, Félix González-Torres, and David Lamelas.

22   In this book, Barthes analyzes the ontology of photography. See Roland Barthes, *Camera Lucida: Reflections on Photography,* trans. Richard Howard (New York: Hill & Wang, 1981).

23   *The Family of Man* was an exhibition produced in 1955 by Edward Steichen, at that time the Director of the Department of Photography at the Museum of Modern Art, New York. On view were more than five hundred images, arranged according to such universal metaphors as life and death; according to Steichen, these themes united countries and cultures beyond their differences. The exhibition featured images by Steichen himself along with those by other photographers both famous and anonymous. *The Family of Man* traveled to more than thirty countries and became an exemplar for postwar cultural diplomacy.

24   The so-called Retén de Catia, the prison that met the penitentiary demands of the city of Caracas, was demolished by presidential decree in 1998.

25   The project was commissioned by Gilberto Chateaubriand, a major collector and patron of the arts in Rio de Janeiro who has been assembling one of the largest private collections of contemporary art in Brazil.

26   Trope's collaborators were: Nelcirlan Souza de Oliveira, Maycon Souza de Oliveira, José Carlos da Silva Pereira, Luciano de Almeida, Rodrigo de Maceda Perpétuo, Paulo Vitor da Silva Dias, Raniere Dias, Renato Dias Figueiredo, Felipe de Souza Dias, Marcos Vinicius Clemente Ferreira, David Lucio Terra de Araújo, Esteives Lúcio Terra de Araújo, Gustavo José dos Santos, Leandro de Paiva Adriano (aka Lé), Leonardo de Paiva Adriano (aka Nem), Irla Silva dos Santos, and Bruno Silva dos Santos.

ART AND SOCIETY IN CONTEMPORARY BRAZIL
PAULO HERKENHOFF

The fragility and instability of favela architecture could lead one to question the solidity of the house, to consider it no more than living mud on the streets. Paula Trope's art, however, unfolds as a process within a field of unstable relationships to alterity. Her performance emerges from crises in communication and technological precariousness, in a territory that, in its condition as deterioration, embodies the concept of social liminality. Trope renders visible a zone obliterated from sight through processes of social and political exclusion.

THE HISTORY OF SLEEP

Grounded in concrete situations in Rio de Janeiro, Trope's artistic production reflects a particular (oblique) history of Brazilian art, specifically that of the 1960s, as well the literature of interiority put forth by the novelist and essayist Clarice Lispector. Lispector's writings on art and perception sometimes resemble the illusory essence of Lygia Clark's *Meu Doce Rio*. Specifically, Lispector's 1962 chronicle *Mineirinho*, about a thief killed by thirteen shots fired by the police, is a caustic reflection on urban criminality and collective responsibility: "The thirteenth shot murders me—since I am the other." What is involved here is neither the logic of the self in language, as in, for example, Lewis Carroll's *Alice in Wonderland* or in Waltercio Caldas's work ("I am you / I am not you"); nor the libidinal economy in which the other, the subject of desire, is imbricated; nor a residue of the Oedipal complex in the superego. Lispector, like Trope, proclaims that the social other is "I."

Hélio Oiticica must have read this chronicle at the time it appeared, as he refers to it frequently. His 1966 work *Bólide Caixa 18, Poema Caixa 2,*

Homenagem a Cara de Cavalo (a reference to another murdered thief) contains something of Lispector's ethos. For Oiticica, Cara de Cavalo "became a symbol of the social oppression of the 'marginal' being. I know that somehow he was responsible for his own downfall." His text *O Herói Anti-Herói e o Anti-Herói Anónimo* (1968) articulates the political program undergirding the creation of *Bólide*: "What drove me to write this homage is the way this society cut off each and every one of his possibilities for survival." This carries an ethical resonance with Lispector's declaration, "At the moment a criminal is killed, an innocent is being killed as well."

Since 1993 Paula Trope has attempted to forestall this death foretold—this innocence lost—in her work with street children, who live in an environment usually seen as a "school for crime." Hers is the generation searching for a concrete Other. A vague desire for alterity was presented in generalized and abstract terms in Oswald de Andrade's *Manifesto Antropófago* (1928), which views Brazilian cultural formation as a process of absorption and metabolization of elements. Who is the Other within De Andrade's concept of "cannibalism"? With Graça Aranha and Vieira da Cunha, Brazil clearly recognized itself as Native, African, and European. The Other materialized when Oiticica climbed the *morro* he presented as Mangueira in *Tropicália*. Trope, for her part, offers subjective diagrams of the Other. It is not enough to state the fact that each *morro* is a singular community. Pereirão made *morrinhos; os meninos* live there.

Critical texts or literature (or music) that question Lispector's (or literature's, or music's) efficacy with respect to *Mineirinho* are of questionable relevance. Is there anything written that invalidates literature and music for their "failure" to bring about change? So many texts hasten to question art and to demand results from it, but this is blind retaliation, a security blanket for the conscience of the critic. To be sure, it is beneficial to discuss the contradictions and occasional romanticism of artistic projects, but is art, by and large, more open to criticism in this respect than literature or music? Successive generations of artists have assumed the task of resistance: Jacques Callot, Goya, Manet, Kollwitz, Picasso, and even Warhol, Jörg Immendorf, and Gerhard Richter. Among contemporary artists, themes of exclusion and oppression are explored by artists like Trope, Lorna Simpson, Kara Walker, Glenn Ligon, Nadine Robinson, Fernando Alvim, and Emily Jacir, among others on the international scene. They use class-, ethnic-, and gender-based perspectives to reflect upon oppressive structures and practices such as surplus value in advanced capitalism, sexual abuse, prejudice, wars, diasporas, and genocide.

The Brazilian artistic experience can be thought of as a field of relationships with social alterity. It is anchored in the fact that the culture of Rio de Janeiro resists the separation of art from life—notwithstanding all academic and neo-Greenbergian pressures—yet without sacrificing aesthetic meaning. Trope's approach has its antecedents in Lygia Clark's proposals in the 1960s and 1970s for intersubjective relationships. She and artists like her have revitalized the generous legacy of the critic Mário Pedrosa with regard to the relationship of art and society. After Oiticica, the late 1960s saw artists such as Cildo Meireles, Barrio, and Antonio Manuel acting as agents of history, working with ghetto culture and moving toward the Other to different degrees. Together with Oiticica, they produced work of visibility and involvement. In the 1980s Celeida Tostes worked with collective forms and the recovery of popular cultural materials in the Morro do Chapéu Mangueira, collaborating with dressmakers and confectioners, among others. Working shortly after the exhaustion of the

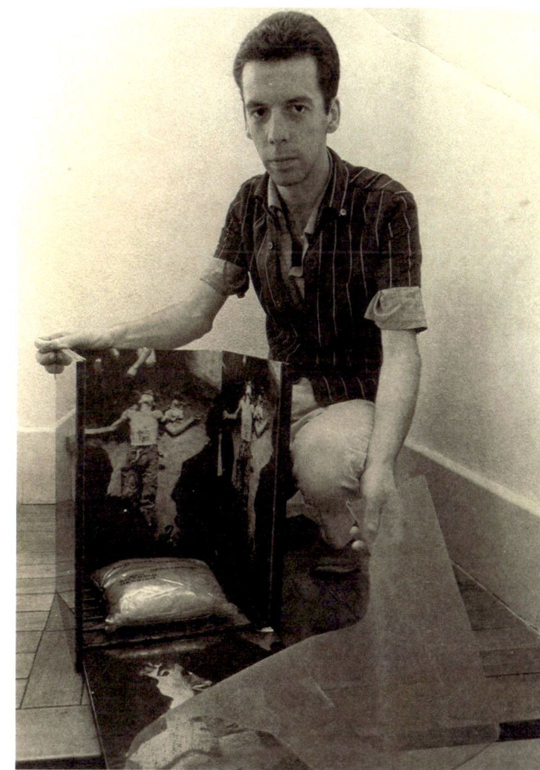

Hélio Oiticica com "Bólide Caixa 18, Poema Caixa 2, Homenagem à Cara de Cavalo," 1966
Photograph by Cláudio Oiticica. Image courtesy of Projeto Hélio Oiticica, Rio de Janerio

dictatorship that came to power in 1964, Tostes took an approach that involved the simple utopian notion of combining individual and collective physical energies into common activities, with the goal of creating income-generating possibilities. The beginning of the 1990s saw a renewal of interest in working with social alterity. Art undertook the task of investigating social being, which could not be reduced to a simple question of human sciences or social services but involved widening the experimental scope of solidarity.

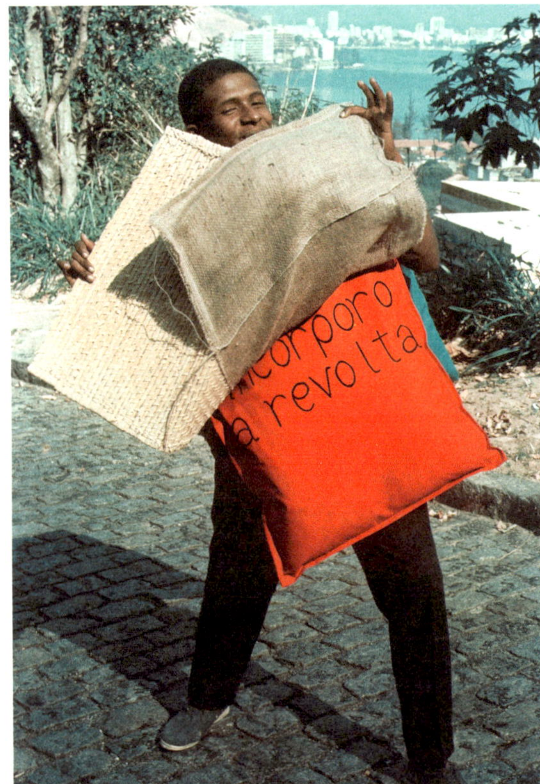

Hélio Oiticica
Parangolé, Nildo da Mangueira com P 15,
Cape 11: Incorporo a revolta, 1967
Photograph by Cláudio Oiticica. Image courtesy of Projeto Hélio Oiticica, Rio de Janeiro

This moment witnessed the emergence of artists like Trope, Rosana Palazyan (who works with at-risk youth), Mauricio Dias, and Walter Riedweg, as well as Rosângela Rennó's trenchant explorations of the politics of the image. All this activity is centered in Rio.

In his essay "Cézanne's Doubt," Maurice Merleau-Ponty concludes that "[Cézanne's] work demanded this life." As regards the topic under discussion here, that phrase can be adapted to say, "These works of solidarity demanded this city of Rio de Janeiro." Since then, the imprint of *carioca* artistic activity is now scattered throughout Brazil. Two artists working in the suburbs of São Paulo, Mónica Nador and Lucia Koch, deserve particular mention. Since 1996, through the JAMAC (Jardim Miriam Arte Club), Nador has incorporated into her work various motifs and visual elements from the styles of house painting embraced by the local population. Koch, recipient of the Prémio CNI-SESI Marcantonio Vilaça para Artes Plásticas, brought her site-specific experiments with light to JAMAC and applied them to popular architecture. In a similar vein, the *paraenses* Bené Fonteles and Alexandre Sequeira established relationships with the communities of Gameleira do Assuruá in Bahia and Nazaré do Mocajuba in Pará.

STREETS

In 1993 Trope photographed street children, those unrealized incarnations of Narcissus, never photographed and therefore faceless in a society of excessive images and imaged excesses. Without any pictures of themselves or, indeed any type of documentation, they lacked, in a sense, any kind of formalized existence. Fabricio, João, Xambim, Muller, and Fefei were thus able to come into their names. Beyond all sociological debate, Trope's work deals with the difficult reconciliation of the image with a lack of innocence.

Trope's diptychs comprise her own portraits of the children and the pictures made by those who are portrayed, whose collaboration the artist acknowledges in the work itself; the portraits are nearly full-sized. Photographed in the streets with pinhole cameras, the children are always portrayed in isolation, reflecting the loneliness of their abandoned conditions. Because pinhole cameras demand longer exposures than industrial ones, pedestrians walking between the children and the camera are not captured on film. What emerges is social solitude. The children are almost ghosts, actors in the social uncanny that derives from the pervasive fear of violence. As Lispector remarks, "we are the clever ones" who seek "not to understand." Once her own photo session is through, Trope hands her pinhole cameras over to her subjects, freeing them to record any object or situation they wish and in the process awakening a desire to perceive themselves through photography. Her political action converts the street children from objects into active participants. This is not about a simple opposition of culture to nature but a prelinguistic stammering. Archaeologically, Trope's investigative portraits refer to Brazil's social immobility since Nicholas Christiano Jr. photographed slaves in the nineteenth century. In terms of the history of photography, they can be compared to the work of Lewis Hine and August Sander.

BAD TECHNIQUE

Paula Lima Trope has a B.A. in Social Communications from the Universidade Federal Fluminense and an M.S. in Techniques and Poetics of Image and Sound from the Universidade de São Paulo. Her academic training presumes expertise in complex technology, but Trope prefers to experiment with stripped-down optical apparatus. Like Oiticica before her, Trope believes that we live in and through precariousness. Beginning with her 2000 meeting on the streets with Lázaro Henrique Lima de Paula (whose surname echoes her own name), Trope has been establishing relationships with street children through video. By deconstructing the camera to its minimum possibilities, brutalizing the video equipment and disassembling video technology, the artist forces images to the limits of visibility. Her antitechnological operations lower the photographic quality, creating smeared, imprecise images surrounded by shadows that defy prevalent notions of sharpness and precision. The photo-video image becomes a knowledge-producing form of not knowing à la Georges Bataille.

When one sees less, one's perception sharpens. Seeing the face of a child who has no identity increases its pathos and provokes debate over his lack of existential horizons. The low-quality video deglamorizes misery. Blurriness, opacity, and distortions of color and sound produce a drama of precariousness. Trope produces visual discomfort by means of "specular disenchantment." As Vilém Flusser says, "the photographer can only capture the uncapturable." This is what Trope seeks to do, just as philosophers and artists seek the unspeakable. Poor-quality video and images thus become diagrams of social opacity and a general indifference to the needs, frustrations, and fantasies of young people. It traces a movement of the subject's libido between traumas and fractures. Trope believes that technological precariousness increases knowledge.

LIVING MUD

Oiticica once said that Cara de Cavalo was a symbol of the one who must die. Trope knows that the streets can offer neither a future nor a resting place for homeless youths but are simply a space for deterritorialized transit. Lispector writes in *Mineirinho*, "My mistake was made in the way I saw life opening up in the flesh, which frightened me, and I saw living matter, placenta and blood, the living mud." Trope managed to keep up with only one of the boys. For many of them, the streets are a passport to death. For example, Dias & Riedweg developed their piece *Devotionalia* (1995) with dozens of children from the Lapa neighborhood of Rio de

Janeiro. According to estimates by survivors, social workers, and newspaper articles, at least half of those children are now dead, victims of their environs. Dias says, "Ten years later, meeting informally with some of the kids (who are young adults now) in Lapa, Flamengo, Copacabana, and downtown, we learned that a great many of them are, in fact, dead. The kids who survived told us the circumstances of their friends' deaths: traffic accidents, police brutality, street violence." Dias & Riedweg revisited this ten-year-old project by returning to the scene to shoot a video documenting this group, the city, and the press. It may be presumed that many of those missing from the works of Trope and Dias & Riedweg became part of the "living mud." As Lispector would say, "Meanwhile we sleep and falsely save ourselves."

THE CUBA OF INFANTS

With her work *Traslados* (1996–97), featured in the Sixth Havana Biennial, Paula Trope promoted interchanges between Cuban and Brazilian children. Through the innocent honesty and affection of the participants, Trope explored the subversive potential of creating a network of exchange between children in these two parts of the world. By recognizing the child in herself, she eschewed adult arrogance; with scant resources, she overcame barriers and resisted the United States' oppressive and inhuman interventionist strategy toward Cuba. In *Exorcismos de Esti(l)o*, the Cuban writer Guillermo Cabrera Infante depicts the island of Cuba as a "negative" map, open like a clearing in the incessantly repeated word *mar* (sea). And Trope, by building a model of communication with the potential to subvert the intransigence of the state, resisted another blockage, breaking the siege imposed on the Cuban people by the Cuban regime.

MORRINHOS

"No, I do not wish for the sublime, nor for the things that slowly become the words that make me sleep in peace."
— Clarice Lispector

In keeping with her commitment to socially engaged, community-driven art, Trope devised the series *Sem Simpatia,* which documents an extraordinary project carried out by a group of young *favelados* living in Rio de Janeiro's Morro do Pereirão. Looking for a way to keep themselves out of trouble—a near-constant temptation in a neighborhood rife with drugs, crime, and violence—these young people constructed a model of their favela using found and discarded materials. *Sem Simpatia* is a collaboration between Trope and these ambitious model-makers (all of whose names are listed on page 94 of the present publication), whose undertaking served to empower and give voice to a previously disregarded minority. In the process, they revealed how the Pereirão community is not the isolated Mangueira of the 1960s; with newfound access to technology, these children bridged the digital divide, producing videos of their work, over which they had full control. Trope thus brought to the fore an underlying capacity for self-expression inherent in the communities of Rio de Janeiro, which Zeunir Ventura once referred to as a "broken city."

The creativity of this community recalls the artistic tradition of the Ndebele women of South Africa, who paint decorative murals on their dwellings, making an art of aesthetic ideals, visual symbols, and social aspirations that, during apartheid, generated community pride and resistance. (With *Universalis*, on view at the 1996 São Paulo Biennial, Jean-Hubert Martin brought their artwork to the attention of a global audience by introducing the work of the Ndebele artist Francina Ndimande.) Similarly, the children of *Sem Simpatia* resist the social apartheid represented by Brazilian favelas, and Trope's interventions serve to make their efforts visible. In his essay "O Estranhamento do Outro e a Perversão das Influências Ocidentais (The Estrangement of the Other and the Perversion of Western Influences), Martin discusses the symbolic war that traditional societies must wage against time, continuously accelerating in an age of rapid globalization. *Sem Simpatia* confronts the rigid, immobilizing Brazilian class structure, as well as the overbearing, top-down hierarchy of the cultural order.

By reinventing in scale models the Rio favelas, each child reenacts, in complex games of conflicts and invasions, the battles of everyday life, in particular the struggle for living space and the wars between *morros* for control of the drug trade. Within the context of social annihilation, the kids create a space of sublimation and subjective resistance. Against the perils of drug use and addiction, the *Sem Simpatia* project was proposed as a vehicle of social negotiation; the kids were both objects and subjects, being photographed while photographing their own work, the *morrinhos*. As both the creators of a work of art in its own right and collaborators in an artistic project with Trope, they redouble their efforts, aiming to produce much more, to fulfill Lispector's own ambition: "What I want is something more harsh than difficult: I want the land."

$$$

One of Trope's intentions is to exhibit the channels through which popular culture flows in capitalist society. In *Árvore do Dinheiro* (*Money Tree*, 1969), Cildo Meireles put on display a wad of one hundred one-cruceiro notes and put it on sale for "2,000.00," a price twenty times its actual value. Thus, he revealed the process whereby surplus value is realized. Trope, for her part, takes apart surplus value and converts it into a critical sign, transforming her unease into a new paradigm of social alterity. One-third of the profits from *Sem Simpatia* goes to her young collaborators, another third to Trope, and, depending on the market, the balance goes to Galeria Vermelho, the work's representative.

Thanks to a grant from the Prêmio CNI-SESI Marcantonio Vilaça para Artes Plásticas, which funded the *Sem Simpatia* project, Trope was able to move forward in the experience of alterity. She and the kids negotiated their involvement in authorial, legal, and financial terms. Gabriela Rangel contends that Trope's work calls into question the Barthesian concept of the "death of the author" and recovers Walter Benjamin's notion, derived from Brecht, of the "artist as producer." For Trope, *Sem Simpatia* is not a game; her goal is to extend and confront her previous projects' foundations in social equilibrium. Her current work recognizes the children as subjects possessing their own language, as cultural producers and collaborators. There would be no positive alterity without the elision of surplus value.

Clarice Lispector deplored the "mixture of forgiveness and vague charity of we who seek refuge in the abstract." Hélio Oiticica despised the "pity" expressed in cruel "social joy." Trope and her colleagues demand constant self-reflection on the frustrations and contradictions of their own practice. Perhaps she might borrow the following words from Lispector to summarize her work: "I keep living in the frail house."

Nicolau Sevcenko: Tell me about your background. I understand that you were trained in the social sciences and moved into film from there.

Paula Trope: I started studying film within the School of Social Communication at the Federal University of Rio de Janeiro. I do not have any training in the social sciences.

Ever since I was very young, I've been interested in art and film. I remember being very impressed with some artworks and art films I saw at the MAM (Museu de Arte Moderna) in Rio de Janeiro, which I used to visit with my family. Also, my parents were young and left-wing, and my house was always full of artists and musicians. We lived with an aunt of mine, Liana de Lima Malamut, a visceral painter for whom I spent hours posing. I think this was my first artistic point of reference. Later, as a teenager, I wanted to be an astronomer, but once I started studying physics I realized I was interested in more abstract issues and had more philosophical inclinations.

When I was twenty-one, I enrolled in the film program and completed my training under João Luiz Vieira's guidance. During this period and even earlier, in my first research projects, I was very much impressed by Glauber Rocha and his *estética da fome* (aesthetics of hunger); Rogério Sganzerla and Júlio Bressane and their Cinema Marginal (Marginal Cinema); as well as by Miguel Rio Branco, Hugo Denizart, and Mário Cravo Neto and their photography.

NS: What was the environment like in the Film Department? In general there was a polarizing debate: one group—Glauber's, influenced by the Cinema Novo (New Cinema) movement—was more concerned with historically and politically oriented film, while another group was more involved in *"udigrudi"* experimental underground cinema, and the like. How would you characterize this debate within the Film Department?

PT: My generation came after these groups. Therefore, I've inherited that debate. And yet, when considering it from a certain distance, this is more than a dichotomy; it involves distinct ruptures with narrative film.

NS: So, this no longer had much resonance.

PT: In fact, it did. I started hanging out with an older group of producers, among them Rudi Santos and Clóvis Molinari, who were already more consciously aligned with *"udigrudi"* cinema. They were more involved in language research—which is a very hybrid field—and in different concepts of the documentary. In other words, it was a group that was not driven solely by character or language research in a formalist sense. Rather, it was a group with a political slant, on account of the Brazilian regime at that time.

NS: This is during the 1970s and 1980s?

PT: Yes, by the end of the 1970s and up until the mid-1980s, the military dictatorship was still in power. It was inevitable for the artists of the 1960s and 1970s, namely Hélio Oiticica, Cildo Meireles, Antonio Manuel, Lygia Clark, and others, to reflect on that situation, in film but also in the arts. Now, even though I started making art in the mid-1980s, I felt much more connected to this previous artistic generation,

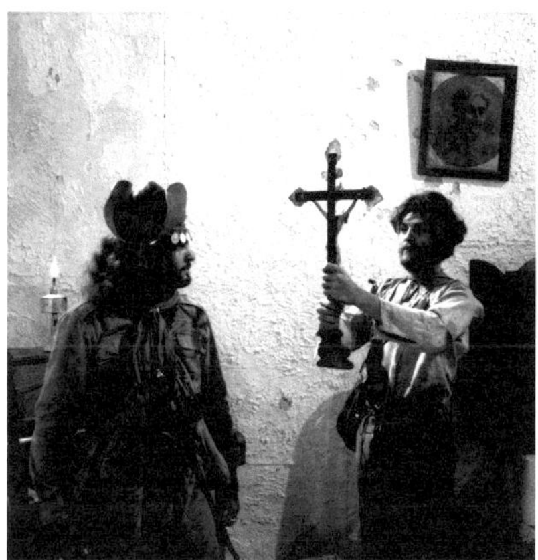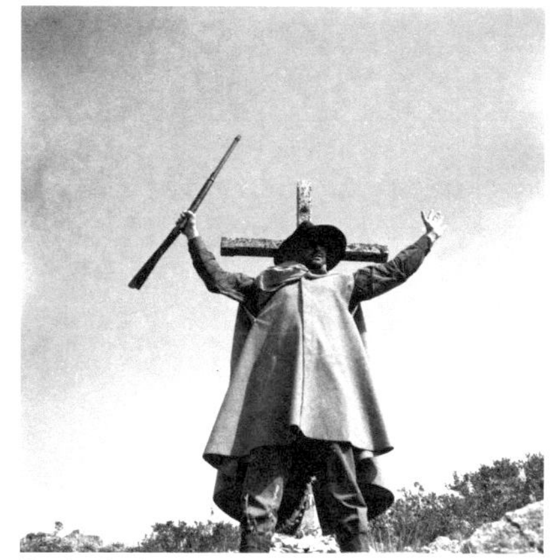

Glauber Rocha, *Deus e o Diabo na Terra do Sol*, 1964
Images courtesy of Acervo Tempo Glauber, Rio de Janeiro

whose productions arose out of processes and questionings that were for me important benchmarks. This is a characteristic shared by the entire generation of artists I'm part of, like Rosângela Rennó, Rochelle Costi, and Rosana Palazyan. We inherited our restlessness from that previous generation—mainly with respect to the indissolubility of art and life. I started teaching at the beginning of my career because my inclination was more research oriented. Although I was trained as a photographer, I've never worked in journalism or advertising, and I ended up moving in more experimental and educational directions.

NS: Where did you receive your training in photography?

PT: I took some courses within the Film Department at the University, and other technical courses like SENAC (Serviço Nacional de Aprendizagem Comercial [National Service for Commercial Education]) with Walter Saint Martin. In 1985, I started to teach at Parque Lage, which was what you'd call the heart of the Geração 80 (80's Generation).

NS: Could you talk about the Parque Lage and what it represented for your artistic development?

PT: Originally, the Parque was the house of an opera singer, Gabriella Besanzoni Lage. In 1966, the IBA (Instituto de Belas Artes [Fine Arts Institute]) moved there. In 1975, Rubens Gerchman took over and the former Institute became the Escola de Artes Visuais (Visual Arts School). The artists converged on the school and it became a real beacon of thought. Today Parque Lage is a very important art school, even though in recent years its relevance has become more localized. It was there that Glauber Rocha filmed *Terra em Transe* and Joaquim Pereira de Andrade filmed *Macunaíma*. I was a young artist when I started there, in 1985. At that time, the school was more focused on painting. Marcos Lontra was running the place and opened the school to some young photographers and filmmakers like Rudi Santos, Ricardo Favilla, and Jorge Cruz.

NS: So, you began teaching at Parque Lage when you were still a student?

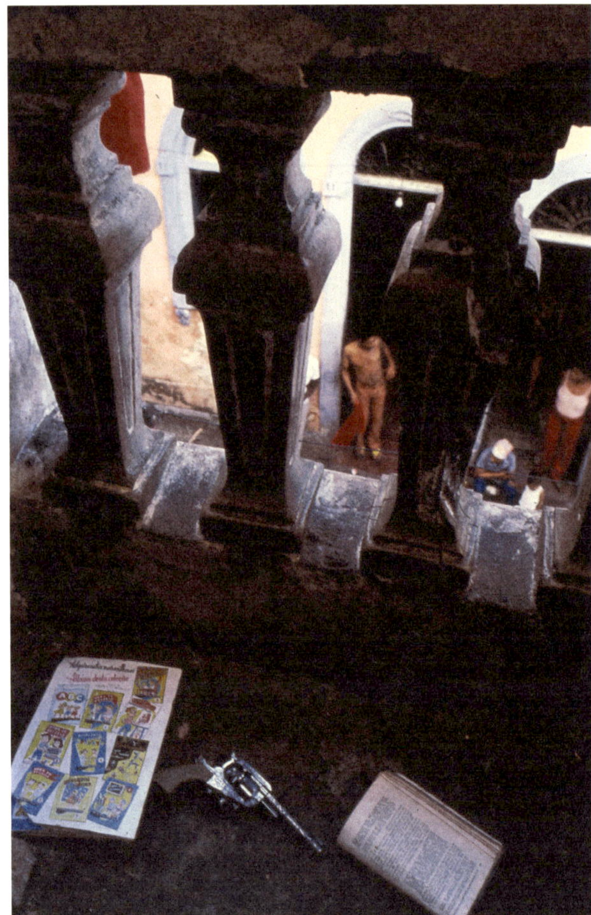

Miguel Rio Branco, *Jogos de Crianças*, Maciel, Pelourino, Salvador, 1979
Image courtesy of the artist

PT: Right. I was still in the formative stage. This was interesting and crucial to my artistic and pedagogical training. It was also important for me to be teaching art at the same time at EDEM (Escola Dinâmica de Ensino Moderno [Dynamic School of Modern Education]), which was a combined elementary and high school. That's why I also wanted to work with young people.

NS: Were your pupils mostly adolescents?

PT: Yes. I worked a lot with adolescents at Parque Lage, but also with adults and seniors.

NS: Your courses were specifically in the area of photography?

PT: Right. Between 1988 and 1992, we set up the Núcleo de Imagem Técnica (Nucleus of Technical Imagery). I was the coordinator and the following artists took part: Alfredo Grieco, Ruth Lifschits, Rosângela Rennó, Cezar Bartholomeu, and Denise Cathilina, who were more interested in these other media than the traditional ones. We created the "Month of the Photo," an event that brought together exhibits, lectures, courses, debates, etc. During this period, Eduardo Brandão, a photographer from São Paulo, returned from California and began orienting this new generation. He curated these first shows. He was also responsible for a fertile interchange between Rio de Janeiro and São Paulo. We were a unified group who worked hard to promote photography, film, and video on the art circuit, and later on we were coordinated by Ruth Lifschits and Denise Cathilina.

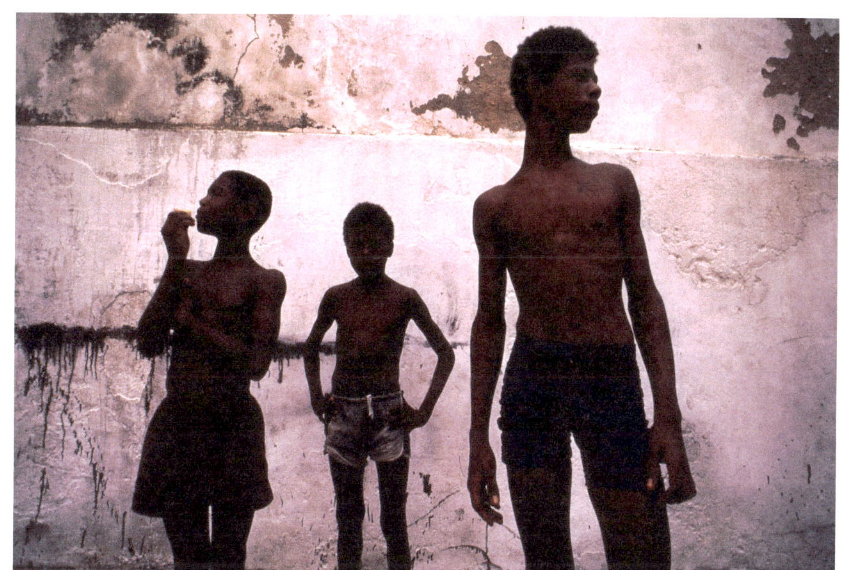

Miguel Rio Branco, *Capitães de Areia*, Salvador, 1994
Image courtesy of the artist

NS: Is Parque Lage a public school?

PT: No. The facilities and staff are under the jurisdiction of the government of Rio de Janeiro, but the school is autonomous, the teachers are artists and self-employed, and students pay for the courses.

Today I would like to teach in a public school, as a political strategy. My research points toward thinking about art as a means to create individual agency. I believe art can promote children's and young people's autonomy and help them develop their own perspectives on their basic needs for education, safety, and protection. Therefore, it is important to pay more attention to those who live in the most neglected and marginalized areas. Working in a public school would be necessary, as well as working in shelters for street youth, which is a different situation. From the outset,

my practical experience as an artist has been interwoven with my practical experience as an educator. As an artist, I identify with groups who are nearly or totally voiceless in the collective social imagination. At a certain point, I became interested in using art within a dialogical process of understanding and furthering the subjectivity of the Other. This is what motivated my first project with street youth.

NS: How did you come to work on this project and become involved with street youth, especially slum children?

PT: I began *Os Meninos* (*The Boys*) toward the end of 1993. I was still connected to EDEM, with its emphasis on art. In 1993 I was living in Ipanema and started this project to work with young people whom I had met on the streets. In my previous research, the question of politics was always important, but in a more abstract way, and in this project it is more evident, more explicit.

NS: What streets were these, and where did these kids come from?

PT: From nearby districts like Morro do Cantagalo and Rocinha. Many of them came from Santa Cruz, Inhaúma, Belford Roxo, and other more distant neighborhoods. I worked in Ipanema in, basically, a one- or two-block area close to where I lived, between the streets of Barão da Torre, Farme de Amoedo, and Vinícius de Moraes.

NS: Why were these kids hanging out there?

PT: Because they came down from their neighborhoods to get some money. They worked as car watchers and shoeshine boys, and they used to beg, too.

NS: And your contact with them began with these chance encounters?

PT: At first, yes. And I have an interesting story about this. When I was getting ready to do the project, I used to see Muller, the first boy I photographed, because he worked as a car watcher. So one day—he'd already seen me taking pictures—he approached me and was curious to know what
I was doing. I explained that I was a photographer using pinhole cameras. The equipment consisted of tin cans.

NS: Did you use this technique in your classes at school?

PT: Yes. And during my years of research as an educator, I could delve into some questions that were of particular importance to me. The pinhole is a minimal camera, a piece of technology reduced to the bare essentials. To open and close the little hole made it possible for the boys to take ownership of the images.

That first day I started working with Muller, something interesting happened. We took pictures and they didn't work out—which shows, by the way, that mistakes are part of the process—and we arranged to meet the next day to redo the pictures. So, I proposed the following idea: that he would agree to let me take his portrait and that he could photograph anything he chose, any object he saw in the street. Worried about losing the pictures, I gave him two cameras and he took two photographs.

NS: And how was the decision made to select or edit the photos?

PT: From the start I understood how to edit this. I had the image, the single photograph of Muller that I had taken, and Muller had taken two photographs; so, the real question was how to choose between them. We had to do this together, but it wasn't so simple. It's a question of language. Although the pinhole camera is a minimalist object, it actually involves a sophisticated process that made it possible for the boys to participate in the game and take ownership of the camera.

In a certain way, the process had been previously developed so they could take the camera and photograph. I explained to them how it worked, how they should aim the little hole, about the positioning of the camera and what happened when the camera was closer to or further away from the subject. At that time, what was presented to me was much more conceptual than formal. In any case, we made a selection, but from then on, when I asked the boys to photograph, I always took one photo and they took another. This eliminated the question of editing. Sometimes the image was lost or it didn't work out, because it can be a wasteful process. But whatever came out was the right thing; there was no aesthetic choice involved. More precisely, the choice had already been made when the work had been conceived and designed, with the construction of the cameras, the choice of perspectives, the kinds of film used and their characteristics, the spatial diagram of presentation, and the dialogic game of the work. The artistic strategies and the technical and linguistic issues were adopted in order to aim at Otherness, to recover the boys as subjects or agents of the work even on the basis of ephemeral or contingent contact.

NS: Do you have any idea who invented this system of using tin cans to make these pinhole cameras, this microtechnology?

PT: By the end of the nineteenth century, some photographers worked with pinholes in an impressionistic way. In the late 1960s and 1970s, there were a number of artists, like Paolo Gioli in Italy, Gottfried Jäger in West Germany, and Eric Renner in the United States, who did some research with pinhole cameras as an alternative to photographic realism. In Brazil in the late 1970s, we had an artist who was something of a pioneer, Regina Alvarez, with whom I studied at Parque Lage. One of her most well-known "interventions," here and in Portugal, was the placement of a large, dark camera in a public square, which people entered to observe the phenomenon of the inverted image. I'm glad you

asked me this question, because I learned the process with her in the 1980s; she created a fine and singular body of work.

NS: She also worked with children and in education?

PT: She had a graduate degree in Art Education and she taught a mixed group, not just children. I studied with her in a course called Fotografia sem Câmera (Photography without a Camera), which is also the name of her book published by Funarte. I call it photography with a pinhole camera, or pin camera. I like this idea of puncture, of intervention. One might say that the act of piercing requires "piercing" technology. This concept is close to the things that interest me about the process of using this camera obscura. Regina called it photography without a camera because of its simplicity (she made photograms, too), but I find that this simplicity is deceptive, based on its appearance. In reality, it is a fairly complex process that involves language and technology, ideology and the production of knowledge. Still, it makes the whole process possible by reducing technology to a minimum, and that's why I call it a "minimal camera." Another important concept to mention here is the precariousness, the "*camera povera*" as Paulo Herkenhoff calls the pinhole. Using minimalist technology implies emphasis on the conceptual question—the potential conferred onto the boys through this process. What is most important is choice, the issue of desire.

NS: You left the boys completely free to decide?

PT: Oh yes, this was the most important thing. Various aspects of this process highlight this matter of desire, and I will talk about two of them

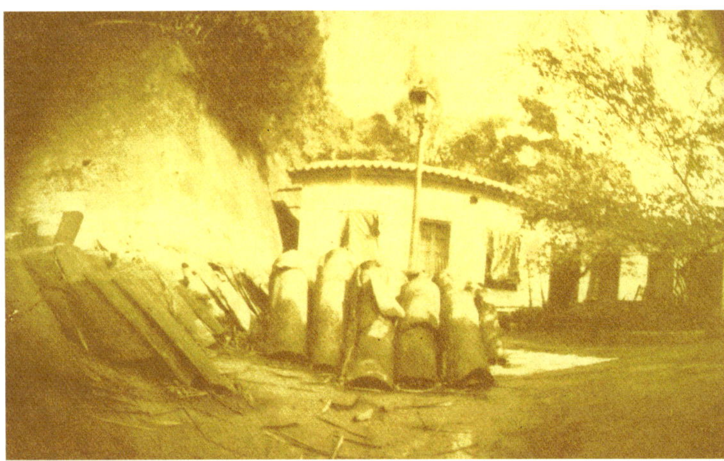

Regina Alvarez, *Untitled–Centro de Preservacao de Fotografia*, Santa Teresa, date unknown
Image courtesy of Fabian Alvarez Welton

for the sake of clarity. First, the camera does not have a glass, which renders it a sort of "blind camera" that demands a different type of gaze. To photograph without a gaze demands another kind of perceptual skill, the interaction between the one who photographs and the situation itself. In this sense, an image produced by means of this photography is the result of a dialogic operation. To photograph without a glass strengthens the photographic act as a mental construction in which the agent "interferes" directly with the space of the action. The photograph is based on planning the scene and on previous knowledge of the entire photographic process.

Another strategic element in this game is the matter of *gesture*, of *attitude*. In this process, what has been made evident is not the artist's expression or *gesture*—which reveals itself in the images produced by a uniform point of view, previously defined—but the expression of what would ordinarily be the object: the youth. Thus, this is a matter of *gesture* transfer, speech transfer, language transfer. Nevertheless, the

artist's *non-gesture* should not be understood as a negative expression of his/her ability to articulate or engage in the game. This *non-gesture* takes part in a productive strategy that understands the complexity of the creative act. Since the camera is fixed in a single stationary position, the identification of the photographer's body and subjectivity with the camera cannot occur as it usually does in photography. The object of the image is transformed into its subject.

NS: And you tried not to influence the boys?

PT: My direction was necessary, because nothing would have happened if I had simply left the camera in their hands. The most basic thing was the process, and talking about that involved explaining to them that there is an image, that you have to open and pull the tape, and the light enters, and you have to keep close track of the time. This was also interesting, because these cameras have a long exposure time. I only understood this later, because at first everything was intuitive.

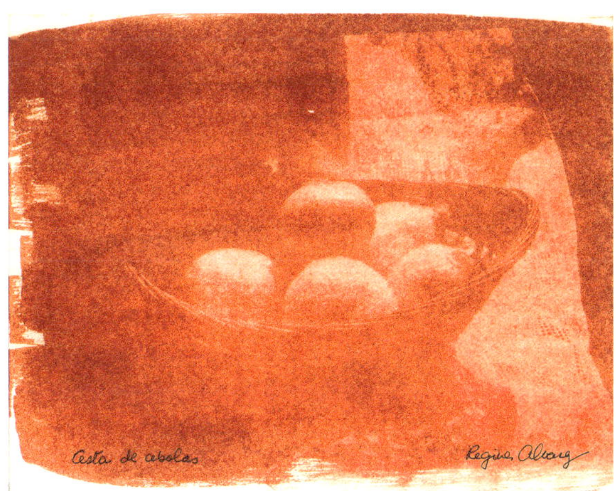

Regina Alvarez, *Untitled*, 1994
Image courtesy of Fabian Alvarez Welton

NS: Does this exposure time last one, two, three, five minutes? What was intended to be a single instant, a fragment in time, a snapshot, ends up broadening into a duration that enables whoever is posing to reflect on it.

PT: Sometimes it took more than five minutes. I explained to them that this camera lacked a lens, that the light was going to enter through the little hole, and that it was therefore necessary for the light to continue to penetrate the film in order to register the image. The exposure time determines the design of the light, so one must hold the camera steady, and I explained to them that they also had to pose the same way. They had to think about how they wanted to be photographed—the idea of the self-portrait—and this was their first appropriation of the process, of the consciousness of the pose. I am talking about children and young people who had never thought about such questions of image and photography, who had never photographed themselves before.

NS: Is there a reason you prefer to work with color?

PT: The question of color was already important for me. But it's a very expressionistic color. I used to work with large-format film whose sell-by date had expired—so there was, therefore, a distortion, an extension of the process. I worked with a film we call chromium, reversed to produce negatives, so that the color is much more expressionistic than realistic. This quality in the images interested me.

NS: Why did you stop teaching from 1995 to 1999? Did you try to disconnect from your perspective as an educator?

PT: In 1993 I left the EDEM and started this project in the street with the kids, but I continued at Parque Lage. At the end of 1994, when I was finishing the series *Os Meninos*, I experienced a major upheaval in my life. Between 1995 and 1999 I moved to São Paulo, where I lived on and off with Eduardo Brandão and the artist Rochelle Costi. I received my

Master's degree at USP, under Arlindo Machado's guidance. But my work is viscerally related to Rio de Janeiro. During this period, I set aside the issue of excluded childhood, but returned to it by 2000, when I also returned to Rio and resumed my work mentoring young artists in my studio at Lapa, independently of any institution. Right now, you are talking to an artist who is questioning her artistic limitations. As I said earlier, I am thinking of returning to teaching, but at a public school. I would like to think about how best to intervene in educational institutions, and to understand the school as a nucleus that receives young people with less access to information.

NS: And it was during this phase that you traveled to Cuba?

PT: Yes. In this sense, Cuba taught me a lot. Despite the U.S. economic embargo and the strong repression carried out by the socialist regime, education there is well ahead of our Third World capitalism.

I was living between São Paulo and Rio de Janeiro when the curator Ibis Hernández invited me to participate in the Sixth Havana Biennial, in 1997. She wanted me to produce a work with Cuban children. At that time I was interested in the question of Cuba and the U.S. blockade against it. Traveling back and forth between Rio and São Paulo inspired me to provoke an interchange. So, I proposed to Hernández a project called *Traslados*, which in Portuguese means exchanges, transfers, transcriptions, versions, and also images, portraits, models, examples. I decided to work with children in a random way, regardless of age or social position or whether they were by themselves or in a group, preferably photographing them at their homes. I surveyed my nephews

and the children of friends both in Rio de Janeiro and São Paulo. Then I invited kids from a public school to join me. I climbed up Rocinha and knocked on the doors of houses at Caxinguelê, a poor neighborhood. I told them the story of the isolated Cuban children, stuck in a place that perhaps they would never leave. Then I put together the resources to take the pictures, and we made a series of twenty-one "photo messages." The idea was to penetrate the blockade.

I was the first Brazilian artist to arrive in Havana during that period. I stayed in the house of a Cuban family, and the first photograph I took was of their daughter. Then I proposed that the children there choose Brazilian friends to exchange the images with. I installed myself at the Fototeca de Cuba, which supported the work, and children who wanted to take part began to meet me there. They had heard a radio announcement or had contact with people around me, and I began to build relationships with my partners.

I went to Cuba with only half the project in hand, the Brazilian part. It was very difficult because I'd brought all the material with me. In Brazil I made color prints, but in Havana I wasn't able to print in color. I brought gallons of chemicals for development and a roll of photographic paper to enlarge the exhibition copies, and in my carry-on luggage were the films, packages of paper, and the cameras for working in black and white. I marked the roll "Careful, Photographic Paper," and then after I had gotten off the airplane, I found that the roll had vanished from my luggage. So, I had to show the enlarged Brazilian photos alongside small-format Cuban photos. The set of photos thus had undesirable overtones of a confrontation between a colorful capitalist reality and a harsh black-

and-white socialist world. When I came back to Brazil I was finally able to finish the work. Then the Cuban photographs were tinted in monochrome, as a comment on the history of photography. The work was displayed in two different formats: as a slide show and as an artist's book.

NS: When you returned to Rio de Janeiro, you resumed your work with the street children. Had your experiences in São Paulo, your Master's at USP, and/or your time in Cuba modified your artistic trajectory?

PT: Doing a Master's degree in film renewed my desire to work with the question of the moving image, and in particular with the question of orality, spoken word, the language of kids. In 2000, back in Rio de Janeiro, I resumed the street work, and I found a lot there. Then at the beginning of that year, I started the project *Contos de Passagem* (*Passage Tales*), which also involved contact with street youths; I was seven months pregnant at the time. I could only go back to work at the end of the year, after my son's birth. In 2001 I worked on this video documentary, recording these stories, and in 2002 I began editing the material. Later, my second son was born, and because I found myself short of resources, the project was put on the back burner, although I'd still like to consolidate and complete it.

From the moment I started working on video documentary, it was clear that I was mapping out the city. So, I chose to take a trip from the West Zone, Barra da Tijuca, South Zone, Aterro do Flamengo, to the city center, which is the most socially disaggregated area. All the children's and adolescents' testimonies returned them to their origins in other neglected places: "I'm from Inhaúma," "I'm from Vila da Penha," "I

come from Santa Cruz," "I come from Mangueira," "I'm from Cantagalo." So, when I finished the project—in fact, I haven't finished it, because it is a project that leaves its questions unresolved—I felt the need to better understand those other places.

NS: During this period, you also started to work with youths from Morro do Pereirão. Would the Pereirão itself be one of those "other places"?

PT: Yes, it is. From December 2003 to February 2004, the pilot project of *Contos de Passagem* was presented at Espaço Cultural Sérgio Porto in Rio. I had decided to move in two directions: to attempt to work in the poor neighborhoods where these kids come from, and at the juvenile centers and/or shelters as a supplement to *Contos de Passagem*.

In 2003 I proposed to the coordinator of Fundação São Martinho, Ataíde Bezerra, who'd been very supportive during the production of *Contos de Passagem*, to carry out such a production with them.

At that time I was in contact with a personal friend, Vantoen Júmor, the coordinator of Casa das Artes da Mangueira (Mangueira Arts Center), to take part in the project. When Paulo Herkenhoff visited the exhibition at Sérgio Porto, I told him I was thinking about going up to the slums, and he told me I was not the first artist to do so. Herkenhoff has encouraged me not to abandon photography, since its function as a recording device is important and different from that of video documentary.

In July 2004 Gilberto Chateaubriand asked me to take some documentary photographs of the *Morrinho* model—a replica of the hills of the city that had been produced by a group of adolescents from the Morro do Pereirão—for an internal publication by the Cartier Foundation, since he is a member of the Comité pour l'Art Contemporain. Chateaubriand knew my work, so he was aware of my *entrée* into that universe, and he's got a good "feel" for things. I went up the Pereirão hill with my professional equipment, but also with my tin cans—I wanted to be ready. There, I met Rodrigo, who told me something about the history of their creation, which they had made back in 1997. I was impressed and enchanted by what I saw and heard. There are miniatures of houses made of broken bricks, streets, cars, day-care centers, schools, bars, motels, *bocas-de-fumo* (drug-dealing spots), and hundreds of little dolls they had made with Lego pieces. I took the photos that Chateaubriand needed, and I stayed there afterward with Rodrigo. Now, when I tell this story, I can see that I was looking for other ways to perform my work, and my art took me there, to the *Morrinho* boys.

NS: How is it that you went from being simply a documentarian to forging suc a close relationship with the youngsters who made *Morrinho*?

PT: I'm not a good documentary producer, and that work wasn't a huge prirority for me (it's never been published). But it was there that I met Rodrigo. So, I proposed that we make another kind of work, as a partnership. Some time later, Raniere and Paulo Vitor arrived, and I talked to them, too. The boys had a very special perspective on their situation, because they were already participating in it as creative beings. I returned a few days later, with my little cans and the photos. And I returned over and over again. I've learned a lot about the possibilities of building a profound project based on cooperation and partnership, and

on the continuation of previous experiences. This action opens another field of operation, one concerning issues of art and society and all crucial related aspects (symbolic, legal, material).

Was I able to make it clear to you what the *Morrinho* is?

NS: Yes, you did, and when I saw the images I was also impressed. I have a clear idea of what they are about.

PT: Although I had finished the video documentary, I was invited back as a photographer, which is something I wanted to return to. As it turned out, Rodrigo and the others had already worked with video, and they had had their first exhibition in the Parque das Ruínas, where they had set up their model. The Pereirão boys have been involved since 2001— coordinated by the filmmaker Fábio Gavião, Marcos Oliveira, and the visual artist Francisco Franca, whom I would meet later—in the creation of the *Morrinho* project. Also, an NGO organized events to publicize the *Morrinho* model and encouraged other activities such as exhibitions, video production, tourism, etc., to promote the social, cultural, and economic inclusion of the creators of the *Morrinho* and the community they are part of. Some of the boys were traveling to Fortaleza at that moment to present the model. They were initiating a practice of representing their own work, because the model they set up is not the actual piece but a reproduction, since the *Morrinho* itself cannot be transported. Gradually I became familiar with the whole project. The NGO, incidentally, was formally founded in October 2006 prior to the group presentation at the Venice Biennale.

NS: How old were the youngsters who participated in the *Morrinho* project?

PT: They are young men—Rodrigo was twenty years old. I would meet someone who then introduced me to another, who in turn introduced me to another, and it continued that way until I had photographed them all. After almost a year I was able to photograph each of the seventeen youngsters. The youngest, Esteives, was twelve years old at the time. There aren't any girls involved. I established a relationship with each of them, and later I proposed that we should take group pictures, because they are a very tight group. We negotiated and worked on this over a three-month period, and finally, in May 2005, we were able to gather the whole group for this last photograph. If the individual photos tell us about their pride, group photos have to do with their idea of solidarity and belonging. Through the model, the youths depict the power relations, ethics, and laws in their very particular universe. The *Morrinho's* creators, and my collaborators on *Sem Simpatia* (*Without Sympathy*)— the name they chose for the photographic project, which in local slang means "no intrigue, no envy"—are: Nelcirlan Souza de Oliveira (Beiço), Maycon Souza de Oliveira (Maiquinho), José Carlos da Silva Pereira (Júnior), Luciano de Almeida, Rodrigo de Maceda Perpétuo, Paulo Vitor da Silva Dias (Tovi), Raniere Dias (Rani), Renato Dias Figueiredo (Naldão), Felipe de Souza Dias (Lepé), Marcos Vinicius Clemente Ferreira (Negão), David Lucio Terra de Araújo (Forma), Esteives Lúcio Terra de Araújo (Teibe), Gustavo José dos Santos (Djou), Leandro de Paiva Adriano (Lê), Leonardo de Paiva Adriano (Nem), Irla Silva dos Santos (Plin-Plin), and Bruno Silva dos Santos.

NS: The idea is that, rather that being contingent presences or passive agents in front of the camera, they took on the image that was produced as a critical resource in order to construct their subjectivity and to dramatize their social circumstances?

PT: Exactly. For me it's very clear: they present themselves with all their dignity and power. In the series of photos, each work—the boys' pictures, alone or as a group, juxtaposed with the photos of their *Morrinho*—is a process of symbolic exchange. The work strategies set forth a playful relationship with the boys by organizing diagrams of symbolization and subjectivity. The conception, the construction of symbolic diagrams, the manipulation of technical and linguistic resources, and the means of production are my own responsibility. The boys worked in the making of the resulting images, posing for their own photographic portraits, facilitating access to their *Morrinho*, choosing and pointing out what was to be photographed, setting up and titling the scenes, taking over the cameras in order to collect clippings and make-believe activities of their daily life. In the *Sem Simpatia* project, the *Morrinho* boys are displayed in both their identity and their difference, participating in making their own representation. The entire work is the result of a process of negotiation and reveals a history of a great encounter and a good friendship.

NS: At that point you had concluded the creative production of the images, having personally interacted with them in the Pereirão, but from there, what was the negotiation like regarding the distribution of the photos on the institutional art circuit?

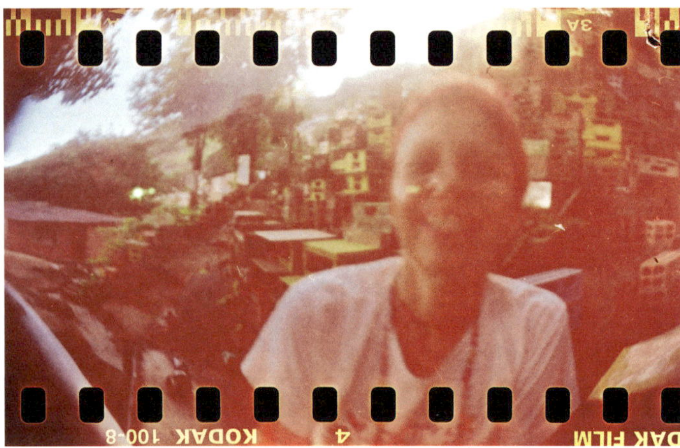

Rodrigo de Maceda Perpétuo
Criatividade Morrinho e Paula sorrindo, 2007
Image courtesy of the artist

PT: Well, we began another stage, which was how to present the work and how they could benefit from the process. This required many initiatives. The first was to delineate and recognize the participation of the Pereirão boys—the creators of the *Morrinho* model—in the constitution of the *Sem Simpatia* project, and thus to look for a proper legal solution to copyright issues and the use of the images, as well as a fair means of payment. This is not a simple task given that there is no point of reference to be followed, i.e., it is a road to be opened, an initiative to confront a problem that I had been dealing with in all my work for more than ten years. Because it is an ethical matter in the arts, I talked to some experts in the art-world about it, and one of the questions that emerged was how galleries and museums can present artworks created outside the conventional art-world circuits. I believe that artists define art rather than promote it, and art-world professionals and intellectuals need to contribute to discussions like these.

In 2004, when I was beginning the work at Pereirão, I was awarded the CNI-SESI Marcantonio Vilaça para Artes Plásticas Prize in recognition of my body of work. This was a great opportunity, since without it I could not have carried out the project. That was when I had the privilege of receiving Paulo Herkenhoff's advice. He steered the project through its developmental stage. Besides being a critic, he also has a background in law, and afterward we discussed all questions related to the work: conceptual, linguistic, ethical, and social, and even legal and material issues.

Other people as well were of immense help, among them Lisette Lagnado, whom I had sought out at the beginning of the project because she was researching the issue of collaborative artworks (later she invited me to show the work at the 27th São Paulo Biennial); Eduardo Brandão from Galeria Vermelho, with whom I work; Celso Fioravante, coordinator of the CNI-SESI Prize; Martin Grossmann, my professor at USP; Fernando Cocchiarale, art critic and Director of MAM in Rio de Janeiro; Franz

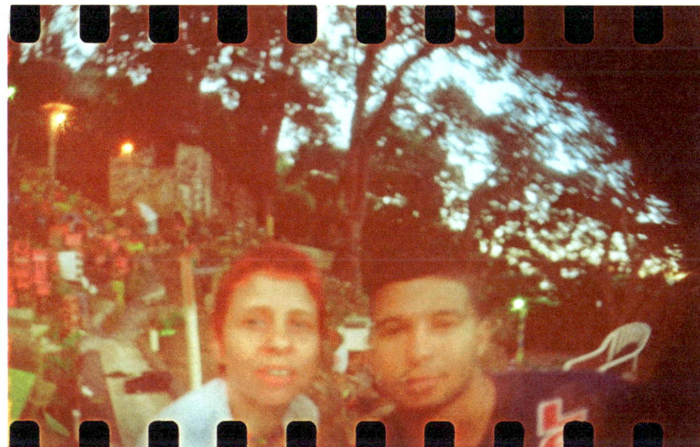

Rodrigo de Maceda Perpétuo
Paula e Rodrigo no Morrinho, 2007
Image courtesy of the artist

Manata, artist and curator of MAM-Rio; and Felipe Chaimovich, curator of MAM-SP. I would also like to thank Gabriela Rangel, curator, art critic, and Director of Visual Arts at the Americas Society, and José Luis Falconi, curator of the David Rockefeller Center for Latin American Studies at Harvard University, both of whom curated the exhibition at the Americas Society in New York City, and with whom I had endless debates for over two years while organizing the exhibition. But what I learned from the most was the process of understanding the terms of my collaboration with the Pereirão boys—the creators of the *Morrinho* and my partners in the *Sem Simpatia* project. Thus, a document was drawn up that recognized the boys' rights as collaborators in the process, in addition to the copyright of the *Morrinho* and the terms governing the use of the boys' images. It was also intended to solve the problems concerning the management of the work by ensuring the rights of adolescents as collaborators and creators, and entitling them to compensation for the use of their images and of the *Morrinho* as well.

NS: I find that this goes beyond a simple duality of "I" or "they;" your work seeks out the the creative interaction of the "we."

PT: For me, living these experiences deeply was as important as the elaboration of the images. In this process, authorial copyright and legal and economic issues were discussed. These boys are viewed as subjects with their own language, as cultural producers and collaborators. We also shared the profits equally. The intention is to provide visibility to the boys as creators and bring to light the problem of social apartheid, a serious problem in our hometown. This is a chance to question such a condition through art. I spent more time living through and reflecting on this process than on the act of producing the images. Thus, the true vitality of this artistic project—even more so than the power of the images themselves, as great as that may be—exists in the process, the linguistic experimentalisim of the work—this collective consciousness.

MAESTROS: DOUBLE DEALING AND RISKY ARTISTS
DORIS SOMMER

What is art today, in the Americas and beyond? Can we distinguish identifying features of artworks, as some analytical philosophers have tried to do? Or is art an experience of beauty that can enhance any human practice, as American pragmatists have argued? The question sets contemporary creators and curators on edge, though it does not seem to haunt philosophy or the humanities, much less social science, where art counts for diversion or decoration. Nevertheless, teachers of both human and social sciences share elective affinities with artists, despite the curable disconnect. When artists reflect on what they do, scholars might find the self-reflexive gesture familiar from their own practices of critical thinking. Yet, academics do not generally stop alongside artists to ask what art is; instead they detour around the question and leave art either to be venerated as universal value or dismissed as ornamental. On this count, maybe education is a bit behind creative, aesthetic, and social practices. Might the nervous flap at the edge of contemporary artistic envelopes be an invitation to rethink what art is and does in the world? If pedagogy pauses, somewhat out of step with its object of study, let us dare to step up and reframe what we do when we teach.

Visual artists have—arguably—been favoring the social processes involved in making works of art, and then the resulting displays that engage the public, over the material products. They downplay the artifacts, perhaps disingenuously since the pieces sell at good prices in today's active market, as if the surviving art objects were little more than evidence of the artistic event. In a controversial book published a little more than decade ago, Nicolas Bourriaud named this preference for interaction with the public over lonely artistic virtuosity "relational aesthetics." Exemplary for Bourriaud is Rirkrit Tiravanija, an Argentine-born artist from a Thai family, who gained notoriety for installations that last no longer than a conversation over dinner. Invited to present at a gallery or museum, Rikrit would clear out a storeroom, turn it into a camp kitchen, and cook Pad Thai for the visitors, who would dine and socialize. Nothing was left once the dishes were cleared, except for the after-effects of real-time relational aesthetics. The controversy over relational aesthetics concerns two issues: 1) how to evaluate art that aims at making community, not at technical or conceptual excellence (Claire Bishop's chiding); and 2) the alleged self-promotion of curator Bourriaud's catchy concept—hardly original, seeing as art has depended on interaction at least since Dada and the Situationists. The objection to Bourriaud's repackaging of now-standard practices means that contemporary critics do not really doubt—in public—the legitimacy of art's ambition to connect creators and consumers into communities that may continue after aesthetic events bring them together. Their question is why one clever curator should get credit for what they all know.

Do literary critics also assume that language arts make community? In fact, the issue hardly comes up, unless the focus is minority writing and the frame is Gilles Deleuze's and Félix Guattari's reflections on Kafka and company, authors who cannot avoid representing their embattled communities even when they want to be free and universal subjects. But let's consider the possibility that engagement with a particular or general public may be more hardwired in literary arts than we have assumed. Perhaps more poets, playwrights, and narrators than we imagine share the interactive ambition with visual artists. The mental exercise will stretch what we do in standard literary education, which still assumes that artists write primarily to preserve their own singularity, that is, to occupy posthumous poetic real estate in a precarious world where hardly anything else survives. Sometimes we teachers forget to mention that artists thrive on moments of extraliterary contact, even when we remember to say that poets since Homer have performed their work before it is published. Listening to Latin and Latino America, the lesson is hard to forget. Foundational fictions engaged colonial subjects in a sentimental education toward republican citizenship; poetry is recited in cafés, private parties, tobacco factories, and street corners in a tradition that precedes and survives Pablo Neruda's mass performances; and Miguel Piñero turned prison into a proscenium for dramatic verse. If humanists draw a bright line between published poetry and today's spoken-word virtuosity, including rap (rhythm and poetry), the false note and false consciousness can undercut any lesson about musicality and performance being markers of difference between poetry and prose. Prose too will have lost a relational enchantment, as Walter Benjamin worried in "The Storyteller," if we squint at the scenes of reading and reduce them to intimate tête-à-têtes with a text. Benjamin celebrated storytellers, like the one I heard in an elegant Buenos Aires nightclub after the peso plummeted to practically nothing in December 2001 and all forms of art rallied to fill the void of other social resources, because storytellers produce events and ignite an aesthetics of relationship among listeners. Novels, on the other hand, cater to the bourgeois narcissism that Benjamin deplored; alone between the covers of a book, of a bed, a reader "warms his or her cold bones on other people's suffering."

You can tell that the disconnect between interactive curatorial concerns and self-reflexive literary criticism repeats in a syncopation between practicing artists, who feature relational events, and most humanist pedagogy, which values enduring products. I once said about Julio Cortázar's best

readers that they reach many of his own observations, but very slowly, as if his stories were slow-release drugs timed to produce a delayed kick in his humbled admirers. Since then I've gotten used to the pausing pace of academic responses to art, and I even enjoy it; the extended effort to catch up is its own reward, because engagements with art last longer that way. But we've given ourselves enough time, and now we can catch up to the relational practices of many literary artists and performers. The irony will be that visual artists, curators, and performers have outrun scholarly reflections on art, so that teachers may acknowledge artists as our *maestros*. The term in Spanish means schoolteacher as much as it means master craftsman or creative artist.

Humanists, though, have been more likely to defend threatened ground than to jog assumptions. Jealously safeguarding the purposefully impractical values and pleasures of art against the push of brute power and the pull of markets, humanists can get almost allergic reactions to talk of public engagement and social relationship. Relationality puts art's autonomy at risk, humanists will tell you. Maybe they have a point, but riskiness is one of art's signatures. I wonder if the tension in "art criticism" between humanist self-control and artistic excess runs parallel to the scandal that Jacques Rancière points out in the oxymoron of "political philosophy," where the first term depends on disagreement and the second on harmony.[1]

Whatever the debates among curators and art critics about its originality or critical purchase, "relational aesthetics" names a common goal of contemporary art, and it can trigger explorations of tangents that get at general links between art and society. I am grateful for the opportunity to think along with you about several qualities of creativity in the New World, its aesthetic effects but, more pointedly, their social side effects, including pedagogy. More, much more, than other parts of the world, the Americas know that culture and society are not given but made—made up. The invention of tradition is no news here; it's a hemispheric pastime. Where European languages honor correct behavior *comme il faut, como Dios manda*, American languages *hacen de tripas corazón*. It is hardly a stretch to connect this quotidian creativity to instruction in resourcefulness. Especially today, the very nature of participatory or relational art engages the public in new or newly framed activities, like teachers who engage students. Setting the theme and conditions for a class that students will help to develop is a bit like preparing participation through an artwork that allows for public creativity.

To talk about teaching need not be self-serving for academics, if the talk reckons with our responsibility to participate in art through the value added by lessons that ripple beyond exhibition and performance space. Attention to teaching will also focus a significant dimension of many artistic practices; Harlem-based *maestro* Tim Rollins is exemplary, but not alone. Pedro Reyes made this clear when we talked about his show *Ad Usum: To Be Used*, inspired by several of the Cultural Agents he had met through our Initiative. Pedagogy, he said, is part of this project and of other interactive installations that tempt and tease visitors to play enabling games. To take another example, teaching is probably what Brazilian photographer Paula Trope does best, when she trains young *faveleros* until they become art-world darlings.

We can conclude from her experience that Trope is not really an artist because her pictures do not sell. Or we can observe that her most developed art is teaching.[2] Perhaps Rollins's and Reyes's double dealing in one

field and the other is uncommon. But I suspect there is a profound and structural interdependence of art (which makes habits seem strange and shows the seams of its own construction) with education (which does similar work). Think, for instance, of Paulo Freire's interactive *Pedagogy of the Oppressed* (1970) alongside Augusto Boal's lessons for spect-actors in *Theater of the Oppressed* (1979). Contemporaries and friends during Brazil's dictatorship, both Freire and Boal toppled the hierarchy of teachers who simply banked information in students presumed to be empty depositories, and of directors who produced spectacle for passive publics. They orchestrated polyphony in complementary manuals that train readers in the techniques of participatory public life. You can log onto a combined PTO website to clinch this case of double arts-education duty,[3] but before risking a general reflection on the link, allow me to mention the spectacular story of amphibious professor Antanas Mockus, the mayor of Bogotá, elected in Colombia at the cusp of its chaos and corruption.[4] The philosopher and mathematician led a revival of "civic culture"—which reduced homicides by 65% and multiplied tax revenues threefold—by turning the whole city into a classroom. Speeches were occasions for lessons and appeals for participation, and his programs combined playfulness with reform and law enforcement. Mockus replaced, for example, the corrupt traffic cops with pantomime artists; he commissioned shooting stars to be painted where bodies had blotted the streets, and had gun shafts sawn into rings commemorating the violence that was thereby ritually relegated to the past. "When I feel stuck," Mockus would say, "I ask myself: What would an artist do?" Pedro Reyes not only featured Mockus's antics in *Ad Usum*, he also took up the challenge to think like an artist for society's sake. Among Pedro's artworks is a Mockus-like guns-for-groceries exchange in the troubled town of Culiacán, Mexico.

Art is a heterogeneous construction; it makes new forms or meanings from existing materials (here, I am Kantian and formalist), and it does so within particular historical contexts that are affected by the new work (here, I am Hegelian and dialectical). And I am happy to be in the mixed philosophical company that the New World tolerates. Sometimes these are moments of productive tensions, as Benjamin Buchloh demonstrates after his move from Germany to America.[5] Agilely, he moves from the disinterested freedom that defines art (B. xxiv) to the dialectical "use value" that gives freedom some traction to intervene in history (B.198). Just as glad as Buchloh to have his Kant subsumed under Hegel, John Dewey also mixed his metaphors about art as experience when he insisted that aesthetics named a normal glow of pleasure derived from any work well done in everyday time. But his point depends on the disinterested, time-stopping aesthetic effect that seems to distinguish art from every-dayness.[6] If capitalism separated these spheres, it also generated the language of aesthetic effect that Dewey pirates beyond the gates of high art. Nothing wrong with mixing metaphors and methodologies to describe the amphibious and contingent life of art.[7] Today, almost everything describes hybrid and precarious forms; in the Americas, even one's iden-tity, as Buchloh says, becomes an open work (B. xviii).

Dewey raised a standard of engagement to rally a public that knew only mummified museum art and therefore remained out of touch with the pleasures and dignity of fully human life. By now Dewey's essay goes almost unseen but for the few American philosophers who rankle at the analytic establishment.[8] So, Buchloh stands alongside the pragmatist aesthetician without noticing him, rueful that critics no longer command the cultural capital to mentor politically risky artists (B. xxxii).

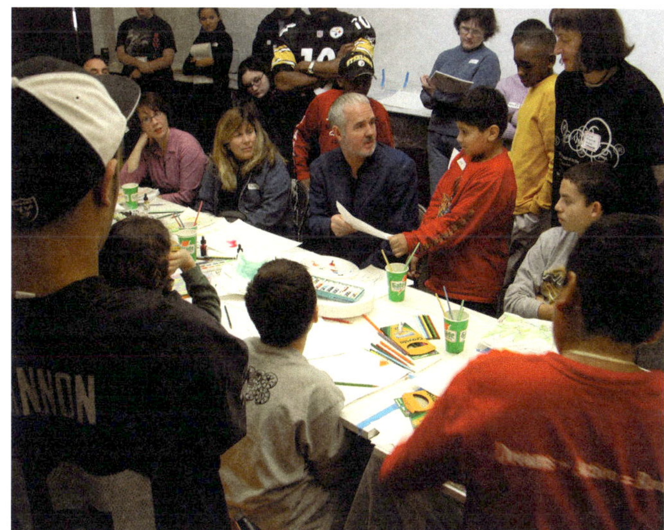

Tim Rollins working with students and teachers on *The Creation* portfolio, 2005
Image courtesy of Pyramid Atlantic Art Center, Silver Spring, MD, and the National Endowment for the Arts, Washington, D.C.

Perhaps the critical toolbox can be recycled today, toward pedagogies of the possible. A hint in that direction hovers between the pragmatist and the art historian. Adjacent to Dewey's dignified mechanic who confirms that art is the name of life worth living, and alongside the artists that Buchloh locates in dialogue with the public, I see the figure of aesthetic educator Friedrich Schiller, who hoped to save civilization from both the barbarism of runaway Reason and from the opposite danger of savage Passion.

Schiller wrote his 1795 *Letters on the Aesthetic Education of Man* in response to the Terror in France; the incentive was social and the answer was art. I underline the poet's movement from collective crisis to creativity as a model of cultural agency. Schiller's canny answer to terror was play-fulness, a human drive that can harness the authoritarian simplicity of Reason to the subjective rage of Passion—abstract form and raw material—and produce pleasing artistic constructions. Intransigent and unforgiving, revolutionary Reason would not be compromised or placated, just as—let us say—the hothouse of New York Conceptualism refused to pander to an impure public that could not or would not let go of subjectivity. Some of Schiller's contemporaries rejected the murderous abstraction of Reason and embraced a passionate romanticism bound up with flesh-and-blood desire. They were less cynical—to be sure—than the Pop Art refuseniks who abandoned objective Concepts for naughty plagiarism that traveled between galleries and *grocerías*.

Schiller would not have taken sides in the art wars. His was a politics that stepped aside from ideologies of either/or to enable both. Rather than exclude possible error, the educator legitimated conflict as an incentive to create, like an artist who wrestles an idea into words or clay, or like an enabling hostess of a salon and a teacher at a seminar. Schiller didn't go from one extreme to the other. Why throw out a reasonable baby with its burning bathwater, and why deliver the infant to savage instincts? A human baby can learn many things if its capacities are nurtured through play, an underestimated innate faculty or drive that Schiller called the *Spieltrieb*. If we train the play-drive to wrest art from conflict, we can steer Reason away from single-minded barbarism and also lead the Material drive past mindless savagery. So much depends on playing them against one another, artfully. Historians will remind me that Schiller was a favorite in Nazi classrooms where ideologues enlisted him to extol Germany as master and model for Europe.[9] But ideological misreading should not dismiss the text. Let us reread Schiller; he is a teaching artist worthy of interactive disciples.

Something of Schiller's invitation to think and to teach an aesthetics of public life comes through, with acknowledgment, in the work of Jacques Rancière. Significantly, his early book on education, *The Ignorant Schoolmaster,* runs parallel to Freire's *Pedagogy* but seems to ignore the milestone from the Americas. Nevertheless, Americans read Rancière; we are eclectic, *créole*, or cannibal. Lately, the French philosopher has focused on the shared spirit of intervention between art and politics; both practices design and execute interruptions of old arrangements and propose new constructions. Distressed, as was Schiller, with the effects of politics tethered to particular ideologies, Rancière advocates openness to constructive possibilities and to an optimism that can stir the imagination. If some colleagues observe that the expectation of social improvement is naive and counterfactual, Mockus would agree, but he will add that without thinking counterfactually, change remains unthinkable. It is alertness to the possible that can interrupt a self-fulfilling determinism which is dragging current academic discourse, Rancière complains, into predictable dead ends. Bad faith is what he calls the assumption that things cannot change in a changing world, since it absolves pessimists of responsibility for conditions that probably favor academics more than masses of other subjects. I am reminded of Rigoberta Menchú's clever reproach to academics at a conference in her honor: "You do very well at critique and investigating problems. Then what do you do? We poor people ask about next steps." Should we scholars and teachers ask this too, along with Schiller, Freire, Boal, Rollins, Rancière, and other recruiters for engaged pedagogy? Answers are elusive and risky but, to the degree that teaching is a dimension of art, it begs an exploration of possibilities as we teach about artistic trial and error. Artists, along with engineers and other scientists, know that there is more than one right answer to questions, and more than two. We arrive at them through play. In the spirit of Dewey and Rancière, play also describes what creative politicians can do. My example was Mockus in Bogotá, and Rancière puts the artful 1968 Prague rebellion on the pages of *Artforum*. He applauds the students who painted over street signs and watched Soviet tanks stay lost for weeks, and he delights in those who distributed pornography to distract soldiers from shooting. Had students in Prague assumed that nothing could be done, the city would have lost a power to resist by forfeiting a chance to play.

The responsibility for educating generations of students presents opportunities for intervention, whether or not teachers welcome the chances. The question about what art can do in the classroom begs the artists' question about its nature as either open or indifferent to paths of the possible. What might "art for art's sake" mean today, when we know that the alleged autonomy of art was, it is true, a response to crass commercialism, but that it gained popularity during the post–World War II political amnesia? Looking away from the Holocaust, the art world favored abstract and ahistorical form over the play of art with its conflictive context. Is amnesia with its preference for purposelessness still convincing? Or does it seem complicit, as Rancière says, with indefensible privilege in retreat from imagination?

Engagement through play was of course serious business for Schiller; it can be for us too when we dare to ignite counterfactual possibilities of art's effects and side effects. Serious play for humanists can be a reprieve from pessimism about the world, and also a relief from a peculiar anxiety about risking professional credibility or being wrong. Scientists and artists do not worry quite so much about mistakes; they expect to make them in the process of experimenting with hypotheses that may fail but leave space to

imagine new forms and questions. Schiller knew how hard the process can be and he would grumble about the difficulty of play, jealous of the almost effortless genius of Goethe. But the work and perseverance, Schiller concluded, made his art deeper and sublime. The visible effort was something he could track in *Letters on the Aesthetic Education of Man*. Its steps comprise a manual for *maestros* of art and education, but the artist's pedagogical letters speak directly to young companions who are learning to play.

1   See Jacques Rancière, *Disagreement: Politics and Philosophy*, trans. Julie Rose (Minneapolis: U. of Minnesota Press, 1998).

2   I thank Nicolau Sevcenko for suggesting this question.

3   http://www.ptoweb.org/about/index.php. This organization developed from a series of four conferences held in Omaha, Nebraska, from 1995 to 1998. The conference was based on the ideologies and works of Paulo Freire and Augusto Boal. Using pedagogy and theater respectively, each worked with oppressed peoples of the world to develop critical literacies and actions to overcome oppressive social systems.

4   Antanas Mockus, "Anfibios culturales y divorcio entre ley, moral, y cultura." www.ablaa.org/blaavirtual/revistas/analisispolitico/ap21.pdf.

5   Benjamín H.D. Buchloh, *Neo-Avantgarde and Culture Industry* (Cambridge, MA: The MIT Press, 2000).

6   Thanks to Carrie Lambert-Beatty for her concerns in the Cultural Agents' Ludic Reading Circle.

7   John Dewey, *Art as Experience* pp. 137, 229, quoted in Richard Shusterman, *Pragmatist Aesthetics: Living Beauty, Rethinking Art* (Oxford: Blackwell, 1992), p. 16.

8   Thanks to José Falconi for reminding me of Richard Rorty. See also Shusterman, *op. cit.* (note 7), p. 3: "Dewey's *Art as Experience* (1934) is hardly studied today, let alone regarded as a promising source for future aesthetic theory."

9   See, for example, a furious Paul de Man, "Kant and Schiller," *Aesthetic Ideology*, ed. and intro. Andrzej Warminski (Minneapolis: U. of Minnesota Press, 1996), pp. 129–62.

ROUNDTABLE ON RELATIONAL AESTHETICS AND PARTICIPATORY ART
UTE META BAUER, CARRIE LAMBERT-BEATTY, GABRIELA RANGEL, LANE RELYEA, AND NICOLAU SEVCENKO

A MODE D'EMPLOI

Before they are published, interviews and roundtable discussions pass through multiple filters and undergo numerous revisions by the participants and outside editors. In this regard, the present transcription offers a condensed and fragmentary version of a more extended discussion among specialists, initially conceived as a theoretical supplement to the publication accompanying the exhibition *Emancipatory Action: Paula Trope and the Meninos*, on view at the Americas Society Art Gallery from May 26 to August 31, 2007. This discussion, which took place on April 6 of that year, was organized by José Luis Falconi, Ph.D. candidate in the Department of Romance Languages and Literatures at Harvard University and coordinator of the Latino Art Forum at the David Rockefeller Center for Latin American Studies, where this event took place. It was attended by a select group of curators, art historians, and literary and art critics, who debated problems deriving from certain global artistic tendencies that have been classified under the rubric of "relational aesthetics," a term coined by Nicolas Bourriaud in a 1997 essay of the same name. According to Bourriaud, such tendencies encompass artistic events or experiences that intervene in different aspects of daily life in order to propose a more participatory relationship with the public.

In preparation for the discussion, the participants were given a compilation of relevant texts, including the titular essay by Bourriaud and other essays by writers and thinkers from various disciplines: Roland Barthes, Walter Benjamin, Joseph Beuys, Claire Bishop, Lygia Clark, Critical Art Ensemble, Umberto Eco, Hal Foster, Michel Foucault, Édouard Glissant, Group Material, Jürgen Habermas, Miwon Kwon, Lars Bang Larsen, Chantal Mouffe, Hélio Oiticica, Jacques Rancière, Lane Relyea, and Tim Rollins and KOS, among others. The decision to frame the debate within the topic of relational aesthetics and its Marxist, poststructuralist genealogy was dictated not only by the type of artistic practice developed by Paula Trope—that is, one carried out in collaboration with children, adolescents, and young people from marginalized social sectors, mainly in Rio de Janeiro—but by the heated reception that Bourriaud's text received from artists and contemporary critics. It can be argued that the debate reached its height in the polemic between Claire Bishop and the artist Liam Gillick in the journals *October* (2004) and *Artforum* (2006). As Bishop argued, the term relational aesthetics is not in itself homologous with the ethos of present-day experimental art, nor does it completely encompass the ideas proposed for a type of art that is social, communitarian, dialogic, participatory, interventionist, or collaborative, a tendency that has been manifesting itself on a global level since the 1960s. However, given its communicative efficacy and linguistic economy within contemporary critical discourses, the term relational aesthetics is useful for situating the discussion within a set of fundamental principles that take into account diverse and unclassifiable modes of artistic production that have contributed to the creation of new forms of social engagement.

The roundtable, moderated by Falconi, comprised presentations by Ute Meta Bauer, Lane Relyea, Nicolau Sevcenko, and Doris Sommer, to which Carrie Lambert-Beatty, Linda Norden, and Gabriela Rangel responded. The discussion began with a brief introduction illustrating the works of Paula Trope and her young collaborators from the Pereira

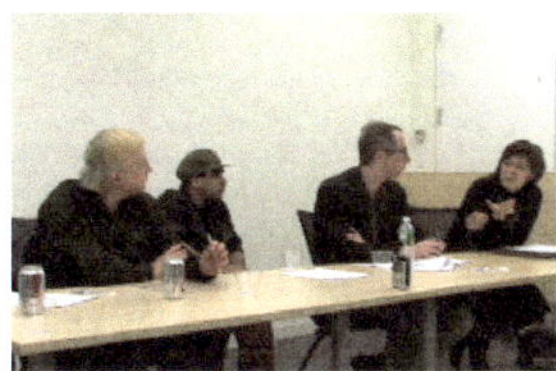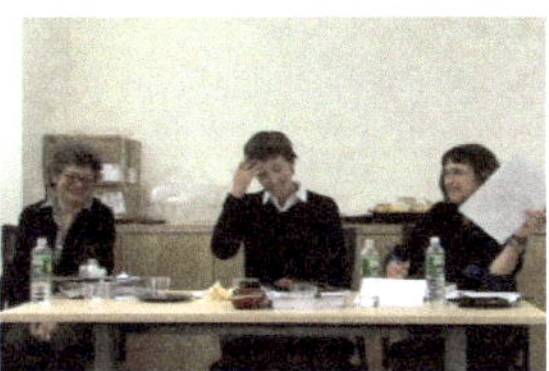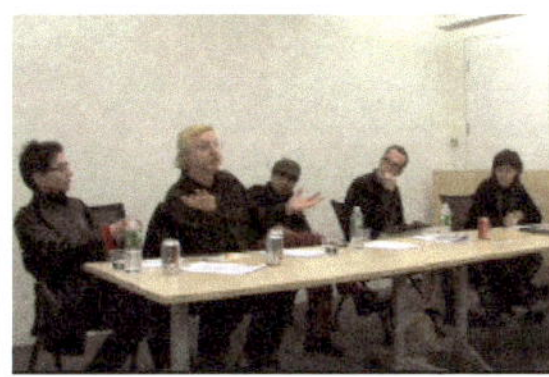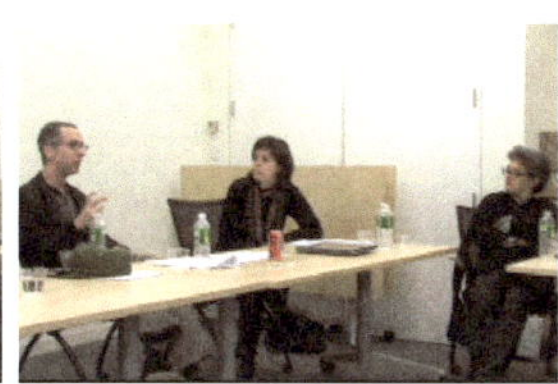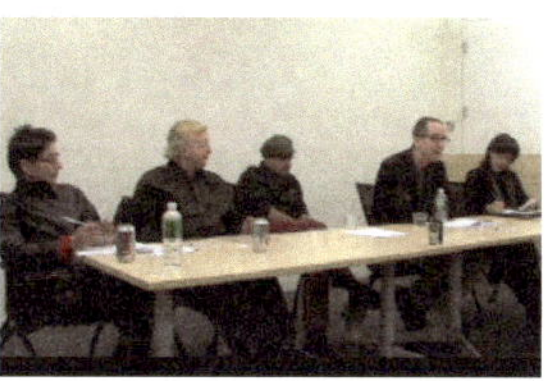

Roundtable on relational aesthetics, April 6, 2007, The David Rockefeller Center for Latin American Studies, Harvard University
Photographs by Mariliana Arvelo

da Silva community in Rio de Janeiro. Segments of each participant's contributions are included here, save for Linda Norden's, which have been omitted from the present publication upon her request. Similarly, Doris Sommer's contribution has been excerpted from the transcript and reprinted as an autonomous essay in this book.

The issues surrounding relational aesthetics and the emancipatory value of experimental art, as displayed in the communicative/service-oriented modes of expression put forth by artists such as Paula Trope, were central to the general discussion. From this emerged a series of discussion points regarding Trope's particular subject matter and its focus on Rio de Janeiro, as well as the tradition in Brazil for the creation of art that is anchored in social and political issues. This line of inquiry revealed a tension between the local and the global, which was explored in a series of digressions from the primary topic that nonetheless contributed to the overall breadth of the discussion.

Americas Society would like to extend special thanks to Ute Meta Bauer, Carrie Lambert-Beatty, Lane Relyea, Nicolau Sevcenko, and Doris Sommer for their incisive contributions to both the roundtable and this publication. José Luis Falconi's organizational efforts also deserve special mention. Finally, we thank Mariliana Arvelo for documenting the event.

Nicolau Sevcenko:
Paula Trope studied the work of Glauber Rocha, the creator of Cinema Novo in the 1960s. As you know, Cinema Novo is a combination of many elements, some European in origin and some very Brazilian, but throughout, its essential preoccupation is to work with a very low budget and very basic technology. Rocha's dictum was "*uma idéia na cabeça e uma câmera nas mãos*" (an idea in the head and a camera in the hands), in other words, how to make art with minimal resources and very precarious technological means. Cinema Novo's thematic concerns also had to do with people living in peripheral conditions in Brazil. Their main themes were, on the one hand, the mostly illiterate population of the backlands of Brazil, the area called "*o sertão*" (this was Rocha's specialty), and, on the other, the people living on the outskirts of the cities, in favelas. So, whether *sertão* or favelas, it is always about people living in conditions of marginality, not being part of society, not having civil rights in any sense.

The aesthetics of Cinema Novo were greatly influenced by post–World War II European aesthetics, primarily Italian Neorealism but also French film noir and nouvelle vague as well as the British documentary tradition. People working along the lines of these new aesthetic movements aimed to create a cinema that would emerge from the ruins of war. In that sense, they had a very strong resistance to creating seamless artistic totalities; it was sort of an antispectacle conception of cinema that was mostly political and directed at those who were experiencing the postwar consequences of destruction. At the same time, Cinema Novo was inspired by aesthetic movements that emerged in response to the military regime that was established in Brazil in the mid-1960s, namely the Theater of the Oppressed, with people like Augusto Boal, Adual de Jano Filhio, and José Celso Martinez Corrêa. In addition, they were strongly influenced by the popular art exhibitions mounted by Lina Bo Bardi and by the photographs of popular street rituals and *candomblé* ceremonies by Pierre Verger and Luiz Couto. All of this was happening at about the same time.

Cinema Novo was an aesthetic movement that lasted through the 1960s and 1970s, but Paula Trope's generation belongs more to a new tradition—a tradition of documentaries, which emerged as a sort of byproduct of Cinema Novo in the 1980s and 1990s. The idea was to give cinematic production more of an emphasis on direct social and political intervention rather than as a merely aesthetic experience. Then again, there was the same concern with people living in conditions of marginality in peripheral areas. These films were not, of course, oriented to consumption by the market; they were mostly conceived as educational tools. So, here you have Paula Trope's strong

connection with education and educational action, once again directed toward that part of the population that is deprived of both economic resources and political rights. After returning to Rio de Janeiro, she herself began working as a teacher, first in arts education in a private school and then in state schools. Her idea was, again, to try to do some sort of work that, given the scarcity of resources, would have to be done on a low budget and with very basic technology, which gave rise to the idea of developing a project around something called "cameris," which we have already seen.

It was this educational work in schools that made Paula feel that she was somehow separated from people in the streets, kids who were not being provided a proper education. As an educator, she wanted to go beyond the school walls to reach children roaming the streets of her beloved Rio de Janeiro. These children were coming from far away: from the suburbs, from the favelas around and outside the city, the same areas where she and her family came from. She wanted to establish connections with them and somehow bring them some of the advantages of education—the way education can improve someone's connection with the world and at the same time give that person a sense of agency. That was the motive that led her to work with street children, that inaugurated the type of work that Gabriela showed us earlier, which would culminate with the children of the *Morrinho*, a project that was initially done mostly for artistic purposes.

Lane Relyea:

I want to start off by responding to the images of Paula Trope's work, as well as the movies she makes using, again, a pinhole apparatus. One of the greatest differences between this work and the new work is that the new work is temporal. It also has sound, so we can hear the children talk. I read an interview that Gabriela conducted with Paula Trope, which was published in *Review: Literature and Arts of the Americas*. I was taken by Trope's description of this most recent project: "Although in these videos the children do not make use of the cameras themselves," (meaning she does not turn the video camera over to them) "in their testimonies, in their sound, they found their voices." Paula sees this as a maturation in her own listening process, which started with the work we saw at the start of this presentation; it is a maturation because of this "evocation of the speech of the other." So, I want to start with this idea of producing speech and make very general (and somewhat pessimistic) comments about it.

I think that producing speech or producing communication is the demand of the currently dominant system, and this goes for art as well. If we can think of postmodernism as having replaced a former modernist paradigm based on quality with an emphasis on education, at least in relation to dominant ideology—actually, re-education, or learning oneself out of dominant ideological sets through critique and contextualization—then the current emphasis of the system is on service. It's on contracting, licensing, and providing platforms—hosting. If in the 1980s artists turned away from artistic autonomy toward critical intervention in the culture industry and in dominant media, then today's artists generally seem to be more promedia. Messages are expected to be efficacious, but more so, they are meant to be extended, circulated.

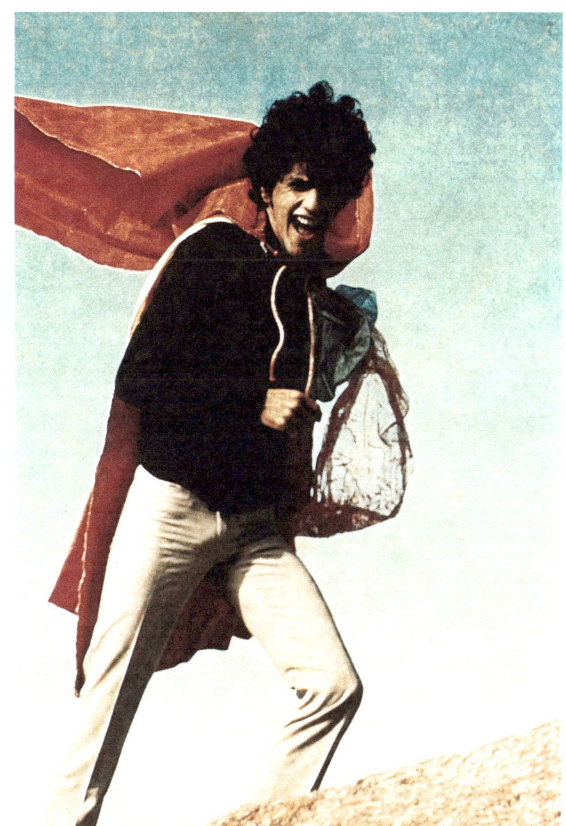

Hélio Oiticica, *Singer and Composer Caetano Veloso Wearing P04 Parangolé Cape 01 (1964)*, 1968
Image courtesy of Projeto Hélio Oiticica, Rio de Janeiro

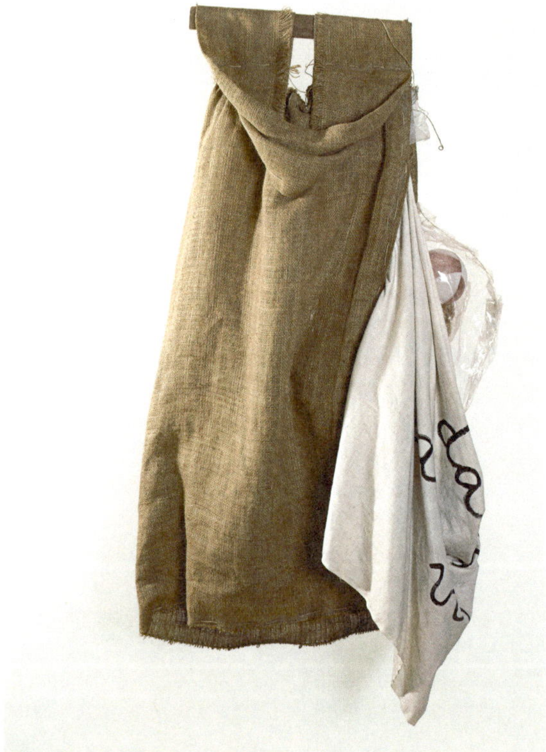

Hélio Oiticica, *Hélio Oiticica, Parangolé P16 capa 12.*
Da adversidade vivemos, 1937–80
Colección Patricia Phelps de Cisneros, Caracas
Photograph by Carlos Germán Rojas; image courtesy of
Colección Patricia Phelps de Cisneros

When I was a young critic, we all kind of went by Guy Debord's dictum that, within the spectacle, "that which appears is good." Today, that can be updated to, "that which communicates and connects is good." The spaces in which art is produced and exhibited are not so much analyzed and their ideological core or bases exposed; they are now opened out, diversified. They are, so to speak, retrofitted with participatory architectures—made into sites of exchange. If this is true, then the dominant motif in art today is networked structure. That network might consist of social networks or of people, or it might manifest itself on the level of objects, namely collaged or bricolaged everyday materials that, though personalized through the artist's intervention, still remain open and available to larger systems of exchange and circulation. Signature style has thus been replaced. If signature style was valued for its armored, insistent sameness, its immutability from one work to the next, then there is today a signature code, which is more like a perpetually upgraded computer operating system, valued for the diversity of objects and sites it can be applied to and mapped onto and for the ease with which it welcomes recoding. Both objects and subjects are valued today for their number of functions, the connections they enable, and the richness of the information or the resources they access. They are valued as relays. The pervasive interest in relaying and connecting, in exchange and interchange, is, again, something that developed in reaction to significant trends of the 1980s, which emerged toward the end of the decade as focus turned away from dominant media and toward DIY media. I keep reminding my students about the days back in the 1980s when the Fox Network was on for a couple of hours in the afternoon and evening, but otherwise, there were only three television networks.

The turn toward DIY media was a turn away from the culture industry and toward notions of everyday life and its pendant concept of practice. Practice stands in definitional opposition to either system—as in anthropology, or theory, as in various kinds of traditions of thought, like Marxism. It is in the everyday that we now locate oppositionality—where oppositionality can take root—whereas before it was located in the political and in the economic. Forgotten, though, in a lot of this glorifying or romanticizing of everyday life (and of practice) is the insistence by people like Henri Lefebvre on the extent to which the everyday is penetrated by economic instrumentality and hegemony, which has intensified greatly up to the present as clothes and food and cooking and furnishing and speech itself have become more controlled and commodified. Social life has been thoroughly pervaded by the economic, and I don't mean simply through notions of lifestyle, but by the fact that so much of our professional lives or our economic lives is now penetrated with networking and keeping in contact with folks one might do business with as fellow subcontracted laborers, as people who are always on the labor market. Reliance on contracting, on exchange, on commerce, on all of these kinds of economic mechanisms and dynamics is, I think, the most blatant aspect of what is referred to as relational aesthetics, and it is suppressed (or you can say sublimated or romanticized) to the point of distortion. There is a lot of talk about this work being a response to globalism but very little talk about it being a response to or actually in agreement with neoliberalism. The nomad is discussed ad infinitum, but not the notion of the stranger as a staple of modern experience created by the rise of trade; we all know strangers now because of the rise of trade.

So, one question I want to insist upon is: Exactly how do we make a distinction between the nomad and, say, the foreign investor or the outside consultant? The values that are so touted today, like flexibility and mobility, are rarely mentioned with regard to the massive conversion since the 1980s of what had been stable, organized, salaried, or unionized labor into temporary work. The explosion of temporary work is a major component of today's labor market. What we perhaps should be asking is: What are the inequalities that structure the field, that underlie the supposed equality that relational aesthetics suggests the marketplace is abstractly modeling? Relational aesthetics can then be faulted for taking a very neoliberal and classical economic approach to the agent or actor in economic life—as abstracted, not embedded. No *habitus*, no class, entering each situation as if it were a purely rational and unhistoried unit. Is this, then, the nomad? This unhistoried, unembedded, totally abstracted, classical, liberal, economic actor? Another question could be: How do everyday practices elude the dominant system through fugitive temporalities of communication and exchange when the dominant system is itself based in communication? Another question, perhaps, could be: When artists produce communication, produce speech, how does this speech perform? How does it operate? In other words, exactly how does it circulate? What does the artist do to shape that circulation? And, finally, how can the speech of others, or othered speech, disrupt this kind of arrangement?

Ute Meta Bauer:
I want to come back to a number of the points that have been raised. It is important to consider that Paula Trope's work can be read within several categories, within the Latin American realm of practices like those of Lygia Clark, Hélio Oiticica, and others. Thus, her work is connected to an existing history. Furthermore, in her practice she supports empowerment, including an educational component, a shared agency with others. It reminds me of the project of Tim Rollins and KOS that emerged in the 1980s, but it is also aligned with the activities of groups like Huit Facettes in Senegal or Le Groupe Amos in the Democratic Republic of Congo. One could also discuss it in relation to the German artist Maria Eichhorn's *Kinderwerkstatt* (Children's Workshop). I see these practices less in the context of how Nicolas Bourriaud has described relational art than as manifestations of a strong interest in the potential of education and collaboration. They are more related to Paulo Freire's *Pedagogy of the Oppressed* than to current internal art-world debates. We should look beyond the recent discussion between Bourriaud and Claire Bishop. Sure, both essays are relevant as reflections of recent artistic practices, but we should be aware that a wider historical scope is involved here. In fact, it is curious to realize how attractive such artistic approaches are to conservatives and neoliberals. The embracing and instrumentalization of collaborative practices is scary. The new flexible and creative citizen, acting in a DIY mode to solve problems with almost no budget, is very welcome. Writings by Antonio Negri and Michael Hardt, Maurizio Lazzarato, and Paolo Virno had a certain impact within neoliberal circles, but surely not the intended one.

As Nicolau Sevcenko suggested, when reflecting on Paula Trope's artistic practice, it is important to consider her biography. She did not develop her projects in a vacuum; they came out of her own experience and her understanding of the importance of education. It is important to analyze the position and perspective from which a practice arises, beyond the essentialist demand for authenticity; romanticizing authenticity is another trap we have to avoid.

There is still a need for intellectual self-determination and for independent voices that contribute to the redevelopment of a space for criticality. And that makes work like Paula Trope's relevant to a more complex debate that goes beyond the artistic field. She is not only educating children in favelas, she is also educating intellectuals in how to rethink our own roles—at a moment when the art market is at an all-time high, having a sharp political agenda is definitely not a given. You can get easily swallowed by the ruling system, as soon as that system embraces you and you receive media recognition. Working with children also poses the danger of being attractive to boards of trustees and funders for all the wrong reasons. You either have to be a "bad boy/girl" or a "nice guy" to become an art-world darling. The "Basquiat effect" still works, in that it communicates the potential of being discovered and becoming famous. Even street children in Dakar participating in a workshop organized by Amadou Kansi of Huit Facettes have heard of Basquiat.

Today we are kind of trapped—there is no longer an outside. Public spaces and services have become privatized. It is crucial to reinvest in a public sphere, and this is what Paula Trope is working on. If we think of favelas, we consider them very unstable and insecure environments. But are our so-called "middle-class" surroundings any more stable and less fragile? We are so dependent on being functioning contributors to a capitalist system—paying our mortgages on time, building up credit histories, etc. Can we even afford—do we dare to have—a critical and independent voice? Not only does Trope empower children in Brazil, she also forces us to rethink our own positions.

Carrie Lambert-Beatty:
I came to this conversation bristling a little bit, first, about the difference between pedagogical and service models of collaborative artmaking, and second, about what is generally referred to as relational aesthetics. This is something Ute has already brought up. I would like to underline the differences a little bit, in the hope that it is something we will continue to talk about. It relates to a more general methodological bone to pick with the whole, larger conversation about these alternative practices, which is that there is a dearth of specificity in the discussion. There is a lot of theorizing and generalizing, some of it excellent, but I think we are in need of the kind of deep research that would start to show differences among these alternative practices. (I use that term as an umbrella for relational aesthetics plus service- or community-oriented public work, though what the term alternative means is a good question—perhaps alternative to the market?)

As I listen to these great provocations and thoughts, the problem seems most clearly demonstrated or provoked by Lane Relyea, both today and in his important essay in *Afterall* ["Your Art World: Or, The Limits of Connectivity"], who has, on the one hand, really nailed the deep systemic relationships among the forms of subjectivity, sociality, and economic organization of the world we live in and, on the other, the art forms that have, if not *emerged* recently (as Ute says), have at least

received a tremendous amount of attention and risen to prominence in a way that is really kind of breathtaking. The problem with writing such a good piece, Lane, is that it ignites a slightly perverse reaction in me to see if I can find an alternate approach. And in this regard I am interested in a slightly weird thought: Is it possible to get away from thinking that such parallels are *bad*? I think there are actually seeds of that questioning in what you've said. What if we looked at it a different way? What if, instead of seeing the deep parallel between art and the current forms of capitalism as a negative symptom of that social organization's totalizing reach, we actually found it quite refreshing to discover that art had such a purchase on what was going on in society, and that it had been expressed in what this huge range of creative people are doing with such specificity, and so well?

If artists and the people they work with are able to express and give form to the means of contemporary life in which we are so saturated, then it becomes even more incumbent upon us to look at the specificity of what they are doing *within* such practices. And that might offer a means of avoiding the trap that is the old opposition-versus-complicity binary, the inside-outside binary—which is crucial when we all know this very system disallows pure oppositionality, or makes it difficult to imagine in anything other than the most compromised way. The call for a kind of public sphere that Ute suggested at the end—might that not actually already exist within the network? How can we find it there? And have these artists found it already? Let's look carefully at somebody's work, anybody's work, and Trope's is as good a place to start as any.

Gabriela Rangel:
I would like to ask Nicolau to expand upon the discussion of Hélio Oiticica and the Cinema Novo because I think it is very important to understand it precisely in relation to why Paula is working with this outdated technology of pinhole cameras, a kind of regressive move to nineteenth- century photography—it seems to be more of a discourse that frames her practice within the materiality of the favelas. It is crucial to remember that there was a major debate in Brazil in the 1960s between two figures: Glauber Rocha, a Leninist Marxist, and Oiticica, who was more of a Gramscian, a revisionist. At the time, the role of the mass media and the intellectual was being debated. The questions were: How do we bring modernity to these impoverished sectors? How do we intervene in or occupy these structures of power? Is it important to penetrate television and radio and newspapers, or should we create a parallel structure, more of a beaux-arts/independent kind of circuit? That was the discussion between Oiticica and the filmmakers Rocha, Cacá Diegues, and Walter Lima Jr., and I think Paula Trope incorporates these ideas into her practice. She is bringing this debate into the visual arts. More than producing speech, as Lane said, she is responding to this dichotomy between two important figures in Brazil. And I think that is why it is problematic when we apply a framework like Bourriaud's to someone like Paula Trope, who is very much aware of what Bourriaud and Bishop are saying, because even though she was born in the suburbs of Rio de Janeiro, she is part of an elite in today's Rio de Janeiro. She was on a panel and discussed these issues with Bishop during the São Paulo Biennial. So, I think it is important for you to give us that context of discussion. It was similar to Marcuse, in opposition to Stalinist Marxism, questioning the role of the intellectual within the mass media.

NS: Your question, Gabriela, is absolutely crucial for understanding Paula Trope, and the way you put it in terms of a polarity between Glauber Rocha and Hélio Oiticica, with Paula Trope in the middle, is just fantastic. And I think it is useful and illuminating to see her from different perspectives, because she is not one simple thing but a synthesis of many things that have been going on in Brazilian or Latin American culture for a long time now. I emphasize "Latin American culture" rather than the art market at large because Latin America is at somewhat of a distance from the market, for better or worse. I think what is essentially behind Paula's concept is Brazilian art as practice, art as action, art as motion, and that is why I am not comfortable with those photographs. The photographs are just a sweeping moment, a single, evanescent event in a very complex process, namely the relationship she has with the children and their community. And behind all that is the way she is reflecting on the social divide in Brazil in particular, Latin America in general, and the Third World at large. In that sense what is peculiar about those photographs is that they become objects and are therefore marketable. And Paula's whole process of interaction with the street children is not marketable in any possible sense, and certainly not interesting to glamorous circles. The question is: Can we bring those photographs of *Os Meninos* to the . . . now?

The last time I saw Paula Trope's photographs was at the São Paulo Biennial. They were reproduced on walls that were twice the size of these walls, completely out of human scale—nothing to do with human beings, let alone children, let alone children abandoned in the streets. What is the point of all that? I don't think it has to do with Paula Trope. It has to do with a process by which personal involvement in a very

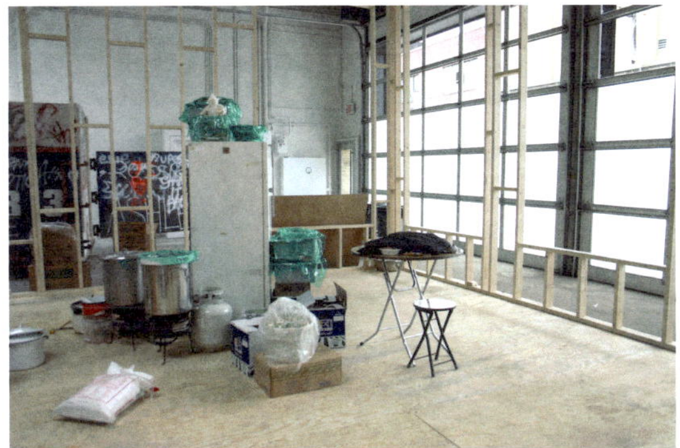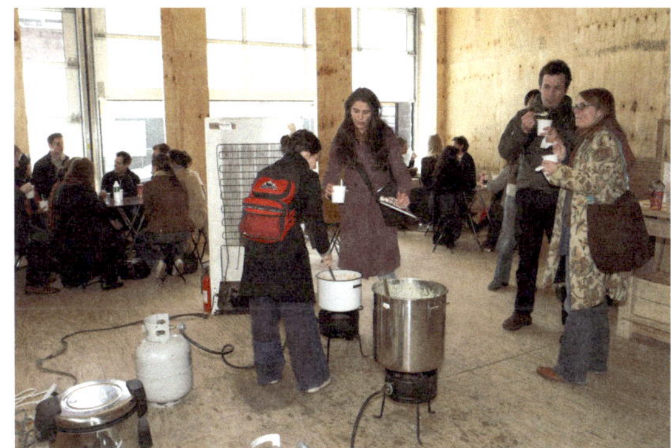

Rirkrit Tiravanija, *Untitled (Free)*, 1992–2007
Installation view at David Zwirner, New York, March 21–May 19, 2007
Image courtesy of Gavin Brown's Enterprise, New York

serious social project was appropriated by the art market and became part of it, causing a total detachment from the original meaning of the complex social and political intervention she is trying to make in the streets of Rio de Janeiro. This is an inevitable consequence of both cultural and artistic debates, as we see here now. In that sense the real work is the entire process, not just the interaction with the powerless, with these particular groups of children. With regard to the complete creative project that Paula's conducting, keep in mind that Oiticica's work did not sell very well, not only because people were not interested in what he was doing, but because he did not consider his project to be saleable. If he had done so, his process would not have become visible, which is why the Oiticica collection is almost 95% complete today. Oiticica wanted to keep it together because he wanted to see it as a whole, as a continuous process from which nothing should be singled out as particularly valuable and taken out of context from the collection.

Oiticica talked about experiences, *vivencias*. With that in mind, it is very important to understand Paula Trope's particular situation within the particular situation of Rio de Janeiro, of Brazil, and of the Third World, as well as the Third World's relationship to an art market that it does not control and that, in fact, is imposed upon it. Of course, people can take advantage of that market, just as Paula Trope can take advantage of the photographs being sold for money. As you know very well, her profession as a teacher is very underpaid, so she lives in very difficult conditions and has reason to thank God when something is sold. But this is not going to distract her from the important work that she is doing in the streets. She is not doing it for the sake of selling; she is doing it for the social interaction, to invest in some kind of social transformation that would somehow challenge the social divide in Brazil. And that puts us, once again, in line with the works of Glauber Rocha and Hélio Oiticica.

Rocha was a fantastic filmmaker. He could have made all kinds of money because he was so talented, and he was fought over by studios in Europe and the United States. He could have sold out, but he decided not to do that because he understood his work as a kind of political investment in the transformation of Brazilian society, especially under the circumstances imposed by the military dictatorship. What is significant about Glauber Rocha is his aesthetic—what he called "*estética da fome*" (aesthetics of hunger)—which was very far from, say, an orthodox Soviet Communist Party understanding of what art should be.

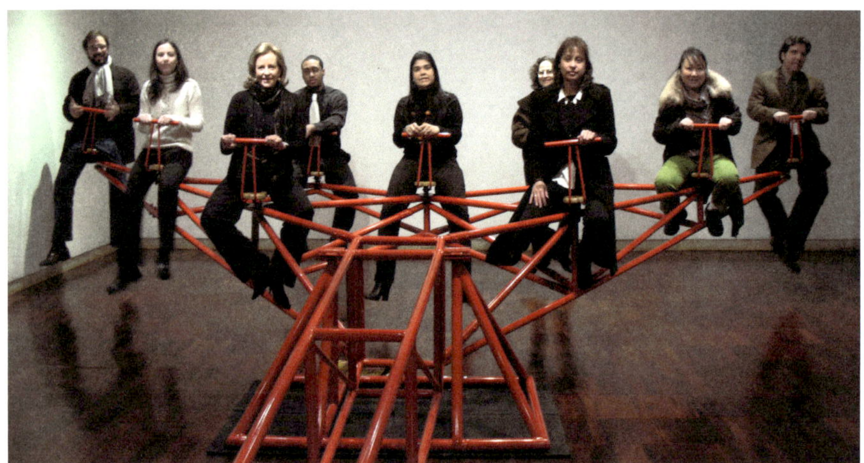

Pedro Reyes, *Leverage*, 2006
Installation view at the Americas Society Art Gallery, 2006
Photograph by Gabriela Rangel

So, whether he had Brazilian Communist Party connections or not, it is still the case that his films were not shown in the Soviet Union, and that his aesthetic was totally antiparty and anticommunist, and faithful to the cultural debate about challenging the social divide in Brazil and its consequences. Here, you can see Rocha's connection to Oiticica. They had very different political positions but they were very close friends, and they worked with each other very well, because aesthetically, they were doing almost the same thing. Aesthetically, they were analogous in the sense that theirs was an art that was antiestablishment, antistate, antiaesthetics, antimarket, anti- any form of compromise that would deprive it of its fundamentally critical and radical element, which involved a political and social confrontation with Brazil's present and past, and especially a message about what the future of that country could be if those problems were confronted.

GR: But, even though he was against the mainstream, he was working during a moment of the emancipation of national filmmaking. As you know, there was a very strong movement, a regional movement, against Hollywood. Glauber, though, was very close to the Cuban bureaucracy and his filmmaking was based in Cuba. So, I think that even though he was not close to the Soviet Union, he was presenting the confrontation with Hollywood in nationalist, regionalist terms, as a kind of antagonistic relationship that led him to the Cuban model.

NS: At the end of his career (he died very young), Rocha was forbidden to produce any kind of movie in Brazil. There was nobody to finance his projects. He was totally alone, and he was being politically persecuted. So, he did not have many options apart from working in Cuba or Africa, and he died of that—he died because he could not do his work. That is why he and Hélio died so young.

LR: I am very thankful for the interest that the Bourriaud-versus-Bishop debate has sparked, because it is a general discussion about general principles, which may have the benefit of conjuring some metaphoric associations between otherwise very different positions. One of the problems that I see today is the lack of theory having any kind of relationship to politics, at least in the art world, beyond labeling or categorizing something as being commodification. Earlier, you said there is a problem regarding an inability to generalize, with using an older (or, perhaps, traditional) notion of radicality—avant-gardism, authenticity, whatever—any kind of oppositional trope to generalize practice, correct? So, there would need to be a distinction, then, between this and a kind of good generalization that can span specific practices. But I do want to point out this matter regarding the play between opposition and complicity on the one side and specificity and generality on the other side—namely, that I am uncomfortable with the notion that specificity is on the side of practice, and that practice is usually where actual efficacy is produced, while theory is separable and can exist as if it were always abstract and therefore much more susceptible to commodification—the idea that specificity is inherently good, correct? However, I think this also goes with the current paradigm, which values the particular, the specific, the detailed. Here, I am thinking of Naomi Shore and her writings on detail, but also of Alan Liu, who writes about how the detail is one of the hallmarks of postmodernism up to the present, and how turning to everyday life and practice brings with it a kind of indulging and amassing of details. We all know this because in almost everything we write we use lists that usually end with "etc." This is a really standard rhetorical thing in academic writing these days. But the detail in the specificity of practice very much presumes a kind of matrix, a kind of big system that is the manifold within which all that detail exists. Again, it is a figure in an informational kind of epistemology, and it threatens or puts a lot of pressure on

the ability to go from practice to theory and back, to allow for a greater ability to generalize from the specific and to take the general back to the specific. And of course that would be very important for any kind of movement or (I am now kind of hesitant to say) oppositional movement

I do think we can be more specific with the general notion of everyday life. I think that a commonly circulated notion of everyday life within modernist or modern practices runs from something like Dada and Duchamp through Russian Constructivism and on up to the present. And, I must say, it would be good to throw in certain other things to expand it outward, but that would also require elaborating a harder distinction. For example, how does Impressionism relate to our current notions of art and everyday life? Here, I'm thinking especially of the great essay "The Nature of Abstract Art," by Meyer Schapiro, which T. J. Clark quotes at length at the beginning of *The Painting of Modern Life*, and he says (quoting Schapiro), "Isn't it amazing how many images we have of boat trips and vacations and spontaneous socializing and picnics," and so on and so forth. It sounds like somebody walking in Chelsea, correct? Or somebody looking at the first two years of programming at the Palais de Tokyo. And he says, well, this is about how the enlightened bourgeois who prides himself on being detached from the official beliefs of society enjoys the image of mobility—mobility of the environment but also of industry and capital, which is the very basis for his wealth. It is a really great passage and it seems like it was written yesterday.

Another example would be somebody like Warhol, especially his work of the early 1960s that uses a lot of photojournalism and makes much stronger connections between everyday life and trauma. Those things, the everyday as traumatic but also as the space of bourgeois freedom, should put pressure on us to make more precise what we are doing when we assign value to everyday life and practice and specificity in art. Another point to make is that the relationship between pedagogy and services, which is a really good distinction in terms of Paula Trope and relational aesthetics, would itself be problematized by looking at how pedagogy is now being invaded by things other than education or mentorship—by some of the things mentioned here. There is an explosion of art-education initiatives, and not just on the level of new schools but in all these alternative schools as well. I am thinking of Charles Esche's Proto Academy as well as everything that is going on in Los Angeles, such as the Sundown Salon, the Fritz Haeg project, or the Mountain School of Art, which is run out of the back of Jorge Pardo's bar in Chinatown and which has absolutely no chance of ever getting accredited by anybody, because it is not a school. It is run by two guys who just graduated from UCLA. And why would people want to take classes there? Why is the Mountain School so hot? Because it's like hanging out—it's another form of lounge, which is itself, of course, a type of network structure. And a network structure is not about allegiances. In fact, it is very much the opposite of the image of the classroom as a space for social engagement. The network structure is a space for making ties or affiliations that are actually quite weak but which are, as they will tell you at Harvard Business School, absolutely essential. Through them, you attach yourself to a kind of social circuitry, ensuring that you will always be fed the best information from as far afield as possible, even if it is irrelevant and or if it ends up just bogging you down. That's why one of the hottest online networking sites right now is LinkedIn.com, the MySpace for grown-ups. It's all about getting professional tips, finding out hot information that might help you in your current job or help you find another, better one. The only information they want when you sign up—a process that takes all of thirty seconds—is your name, your date of birth, and the names of the schools you went to. And then you are "linked in," which means that the school is an automatic mechanism for creating networks of weak ties.

We know there is information that is just hard data; it goes anywhere and just is what it is. It is handled by people in data-entry jobs. And then there are data that need to be interpreted, evaluated, and judged, which requires a lot more work and pays higher salaries. So, we might not get paid a whole lot, but as far as things are going in the economy, it's not bad to be on this analytical side of information, rather than simply stacking it into places. However, in our line of work, there is a greater need for face-to-face situations. You need to bounce things off of people, you need to get other people's input, and that is why people working within sectors like education, but also in art, curating, and so on, have these kinds of social ties. It is not bound to any one city; it is not bound to a neighborhood; it is not a union or anything like that. It is a shared set of itineraries, of institutions. And these kinds of networks are precisely neoliberal in that they are weakly affiliated, filled with people doing their own projects who are usually subcontracted because they are valued for having their own specialties, and this really atomizes a labor field. I still think that we really are in opposition to capitalism in its current form, which is neoliberal because it wants to make everybody into his or her own agent. Finally, if pedagogy is itself becoming more and more a site for producing networks, which are so important for the information economy, then even if you do go back to a more hardcore notion of pedagogy, the question remains of whether you should choose between community or dissensus, in the sense that Bill Readings discusses in *The University in Ruins*. But it's not just him; other people have been trying to theorize a pedagogical scene that would allow for singularity—otherness—as a way to condition the idea or possibilities of communication. Thus, the one thing one does not allow for in the pedagogical scene is slipping into some kind of apriority that assumes we are all able to communicate, that we are all going to be able to understand, and that something consensual is going to come out of this.

UMB: Back to the alternative, which we discussed earlier. Asked in an interview by Hans Ulrich Obrist about how she feels about her antitheater, Nathalie Sarraute answered, "There is no such thing as antitheater; there is only theater." We have access to different categories of (airport) lounges, and although we inhabit different social topographies based on class segregations, we nevertheless share the same planet, the same environment. Class, gender, and ethnic distinctions can only occur within a shared competitive territory. It is no different in the art world: artists, no matter what or at which end they work on, contribute to the same art world. Thus, it is important to know your system of reference and to invest in a proper contextualization. During Oiticica's time it was possible to step out of the (art) institution. Today, matters are slightly different: there is no way out. To escape the art system, you have to leave it for good. To come back to what you said, Nicolau—this might surprise you, but Latin America and Communist-run China have the fastest-growing art markets.

NS: Well, you have artists and artists. You have art schools and art schools. . . .

GR: I don't think Paula Trope is in that art world, but she is aware of that art world. She is part of that system.

UMB: We might be very critical and think we are not part of this art system, but we are nevertheless incorporated. We have less control than in the past over where we are situated and how we are read and understood. Although I teach at a university, my work is still reflected in the art system, and so is Paula Trope's. She contributes to art events and her work is shown at biennials. That is not being outside of the art world, although she might be very aware of the implications.

NS: I think we can play with the system but not necessarily according to the rules.

UMB: I didn't say that she played according to the rules, I just stated that we all participate in that same system whether we like it or not. Trope is not an outsider; even if her practice is located at a distance from the center, in a so-called developing country, the reception occurs here, within an art-historical canon. You said it was a question of how we operate in the system. Although what we have today is a faster, more widespread network of dissemination, it is still controlled by a few. What feeds the art system now comes from more distant and sometimes more exotic locations, like the food and other goods we consume. It is called globalization. Unfortunately, most of the time it is the same old dominant canon, except with a greater reach.

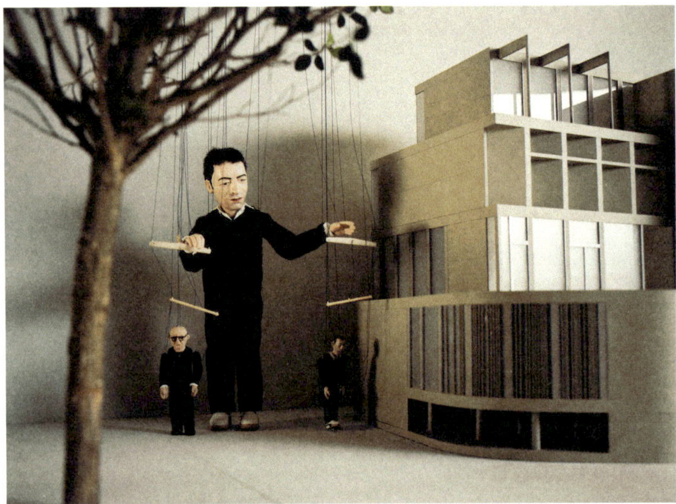

Pierre Huyghe, *This Is Not a Time for Dreaming*, 2004
Image courtesy of Marian Goodman Gallery, New York

It would be interesting to read Trope's practice with an eye on some artistic movements of the last century, from Dadaism to Surrealism, the Situationists and Fluxus, the Gutai group in Japan, etc. Latin America had a very strong, politically engaged art scene, particularly after World War II, as there was migration back and forth to Europe. The whole history of colonialism and postcolonialism, and the notion of Creole practices, come to mind: the influence of Frantz Fanon's *The Wretched of the Earth* and *Black Skin, White Masks* and the impact of, and resistance to, the Latin American dictatorships. These are important historical developments that formed specific discourses and practices, but again, that did not take place in some mysterious "outside." Today, the art world celebrates philosophers of the season: one year it is Negri and Hardt, the next it is Giorgio Agamben and Alain Badiou, and now it is Jacques Rancière. Relevant projects take place within both mainstream institutions and so-called alternative spaces. I meet conservatives in both fields. Sure, it is crucial to reflect more in-depth individual artistic practices and to carry out proper research. And the opportunity to debate a single artistic position in a group like ours today, over several hours, has indeed become an exception.

GR: There is something we have not considered: the role of modern cinema. I'm not talking about historical cinema or the specific debate between Rocha or Oiticica, but about the impact of *Cidade de Deus* (*City of God*) as the model for representing the Third World. You have that in Brazil, and you have *Amores Perros*, its equivalent in Mexico, and other examples from the periphery. I find it discouraging that *Pixote* or *Cidade de Deus* has the power to replicate the conditions of exploitation by presenting the destitute as just somehow being there. And I think it is very interesting that Paula's work functions as a model for doing the opposite, for co-opting the stereotypes in order to bring a modicum of democracy to people who are misrepresented or represented as merely an abstract parallel structure, a fringe within a society that was never modernized.

UMB: You are right; it is about insisting on some sort of democracy, some participatory options similar to what I experienced in a community in Tijuana. The desire for empowerment develops internal leadership, and of course, this creates internal power structures. Nevertheless, I witnessed a very good sense of self-regulation.

GR: I agree with you to some extent, but, you know, recuperating a tourist market that is not in the hands of the favela is something I find very interesting as a form of resistance.

LR: But you want at least to contextualize it. You want to condition what you mean by resistance. You want to qualify what you mean by entrepreneurs being guerrillas or free agents, because this is exactly how a lot of work has been done over the last ten years or so—to basically promote the conversion of the labor force into temporary labor. Daniel Pink, Al Gore's speechwriter, wrote this manifesto called *Free Agent Nation*, and it sounded great. They're using artists as the poster children to promote this sort of entrepreneurialism. Andrew Ross writes about it in *No Collar*, but a lot of other people do, too, and it is something that should be of concern, because even if you don't want to rely on avant-garde models of artistic righteousness, you can at least extract from Marxism something that sounds a whole lot more absolute: that the image of the artwork—the image of the artist—is an image of free labor. I don't think we are past the day when that is the case, and that should haunt us. This should be oppositional in and of itself, this notion that after all the labor is expended on taking care of external needs— heat, shelter, food, and so on—labor is going to be freer. It is going to externalize or concretize something about the human that is not about

animal necessity. And you can take that, like maybe Paula Trope does, and choose to instrumentalize it yourself, use it to reform or ameliorate this or that social problem, or you can choose not to. I think the example of Santiago Sierra is really interesting, because there you see similar figures, people who usually have a different legal status but who, like the kids at the favela, don't have Trope's or our degree of flexibility and mobility. These are actual nomads who might be harassed under most immigration law. The kids in the favela, though homeless and nomadic, are still very much pinned down by certain conditions and determinants. And the thing about the money they earn is that they're distinguishing between the kinds of capital that comes out of an artwork, making it clear that economic capital is not the only kind. When you really reduce it down, it is very crude.

CLB: And I think that is precisely the problem with a certain tendency to say—as I myself did before—that there is the market and then there is the other stuff, because the big lesson of exactly the kind of material you've been bringing out is that there is a kind of continuity between cultural capital and economic capital that is completely permeable.

UMB: But there is a danger of unintended commodification, of becoming a service provider. If we return to Paulo Freire's *Pedagogy of the Oppressed*, we see that there is a potential empowerment that education can provide. If you can raise your voice, you might be heard. If you learn to understand the structural problematic of your situation, you are able to develop a strategy. When you realize that, as an individual, you are a powerless victim of a system, you realize the need to join forces with others and to form a community of shared interests. When

you understand the mechanisms of the system, you are able to inter-
fere, to resist, to develop an "alternative." I agree that Paula Trope's
work is to be situated in such a context. She introduces others to an
option to become active, an option that worked for her. Her practice
arises out of her own experience, and that is crucial. And, as mentioned
earlier, we find similar practices in other parts of the world, such as Le
Groupe Amos in Kinshasa and Huit Facettes in Dakar, that are
embedded in a specific community. When they become "mediatized,"
misunderstandings occur quickly. We went through this as curators of
Documenta 11. For example, Thomas Hirschhorn's work is often
completely misinterpreted. He is seen as someone with an engagement
in low-income, working-class, or immigrant neighborhoods, although he
has stated clearly that he works there as an artist who is interested in
such topographies in order to situate his art, not to serve as a social
worker in a conventional sense.

GR: Critical Art Ensemble is a very good example of that. They directly
use the word "sociology" in their practice. They define themselves as
sociologists, which is a very interesting trope in this model of social
agency within the museum.

LR: The way these kids in the favela are described is a Marxist dream.
It is not that you don't work or that there is no work, but that you can
reconcile need with creativity—you can make it beautiful. You can
make it into a work of art. And they do that, according to some people.
Some other people would say, "I don't want to sell short the dream of
art. I don't want to use it to perfume what is actually a pretty unfree
situation that creates those kinds of conditions."

CLB: Works of art do things out in the world, and they work through
social conditions. To say that they work *through* them is different from
saying that they manifest or demonstrate or are complicit *with* them.

And so, all of these socially oriented or participatory or community-
based projects could be understood as experiments that simultaneously
work toward the good with individuals in a really localized situation *and*
work through some of the social contradictions, problems, and new
models of the realities in which we are living.

UMB: Again, we have to be clear. These are artists; they feel part of a
community, and they do their work like everyone else in the community.
But one of the art system's inherent mechanisms is to single out individuals. Value in the art world is based on being outstanding, not a part of
something. As soon as an artist is reviewed in *Artforum*, for example,
he or she is separated from a community, whereas most people work for
years and never even make it into their local newspaper. Take Joseph
Beuys, for example. It is difficult for artists to be a part of society like
everyone else; they have a specific function.

If you take the example of *Food* by Gordon Matta-Clark and his peers,
they didn't run the place to introduce an alternative practice to the art
press but because there were hardly any restaurants in Soho at that
time. Food was part of their daily life. Today, we are so dependent on
being recognized and so conditioned by the media that if something is
not immediately mediatized, it's like it does not exist.

NS: First, the market is broad, strong, and infinitely capable of assimilating anything it bumps into. Nobody is going to discuss it, that's for sure. It is absolutely out of the question. The second thing is, people want to be part of this art market because of the advantages you can take from it if you are somehow connected to it. Now, other people in the world for whom empowerment is more important than any single art object or installation or intervention necessarily have to be integrated into that market. What I mean is, should we judge Paula Trope's work for what the market considers interesting about it or for what she herself considers interesting? There is a difference between Paula Trope and Galeria Vermelho. Galeria Vermelho is her agent. I think one of the reasons why the Latin American market is enjoying an upsurge in the art world is not only because it is so incredibly professional and competent, but because even someone like Paula Trope can be promoted by it. The reason I saw Paula Trope's huge panels in the São Paulo Biennial is because of Galeria Vermelho, not because of her. The reason she is in the Venice Biennale now is because of Galeria Vermelho, not because of the work she does in the streets of Rio de Janeiro with children who are not very receptive to—indeed, are resistant to—someone treating them nicely, simply because nobody else in the world does that and they don't know how to react. So, to do this kind of work is extremely difficult. It takes a long, long time to earn the children's trust, and you must invest a lot of time in that relationship in order to get something out of it. And that is not going to be a matter of a few pictures—of course it is more than that—but what can make situations like that exist is the selling of the photographs. In that sense, do ordinary people have a right to make art or is it just a monopoly of professional artists in the market? Shall we bow to that monopoly or shall we accept that someone can engage in artistic activities that give them the power to see the work from their own perspective, and, more, to assume that their perspective is as legitimate as any other in the world? That is what is truly relevant about Paula Trope, not the photographs themselves.

WORKS

Paula Trope in collaboration with Muller

Panel 1:
Muller, aos 8 anos, guardador de carros
(*Muller, 8 years old, watcher of cars*)
53.5 x 42.3 ins.

Panel 2:
Sem título (O dinheiro)
(*Untitled [Money]*)
14.8 x 24.2 ins.

From the series *Os Meninos* (*The Boys*), 1993–94
Pinhole camera photography on colored resin paper
Collection of the artist, Rio de Janeiro

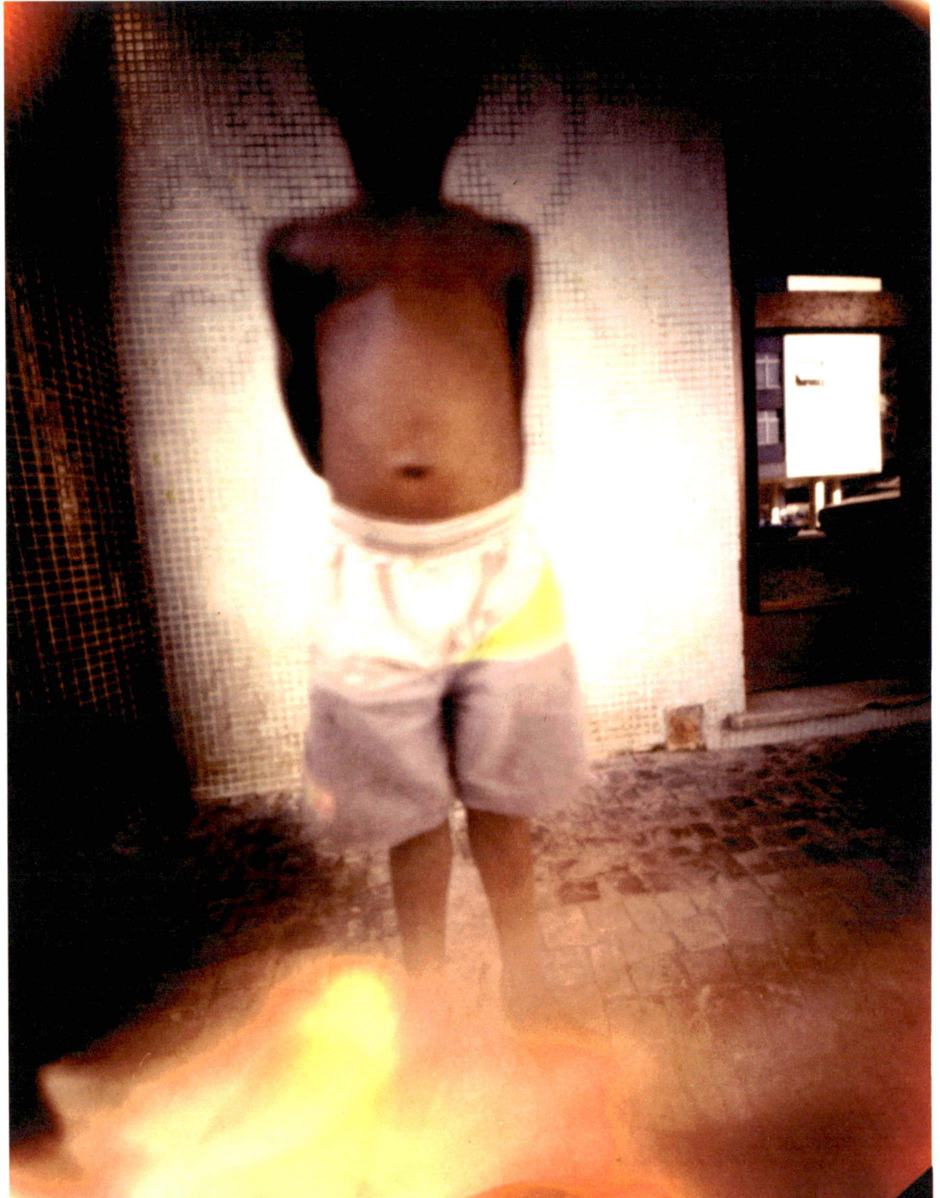

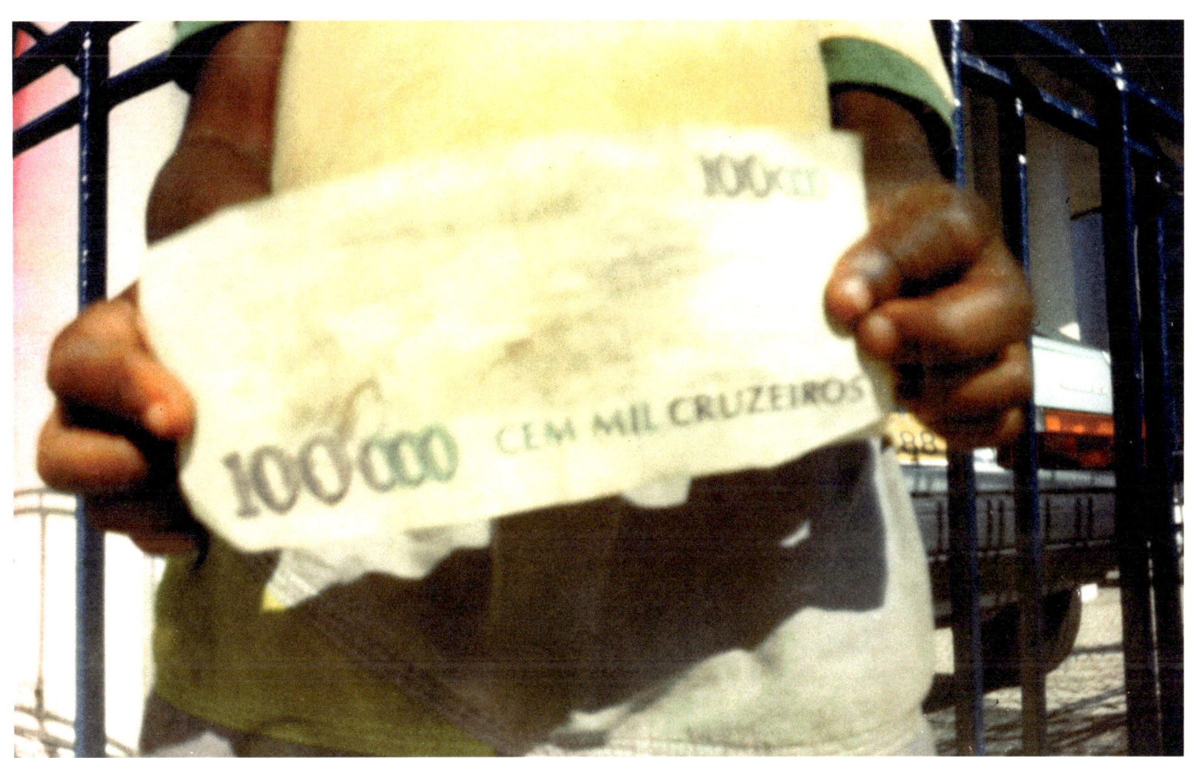
100000
100 000 CEM MIL CRUZEIROS

Paula Trope in collaboration with
Fabrício, Júlio, and Xambim (Dângelo)

Panel 1:
Fabrício, Júlio, e Xambim (Dângelo)
53.5 x 42.3 ins.

Panel 2:
Sem título (A vitrine)
(*Untitled [The Display Window]*)
16.5 x 24 ins.

From the series *Os Meninos* (*The Boys*), 1993–94
Pinhole camera photography on colored resin paper
Coleção Gilberto Chateaubriand,
Museu de Arte Moderna, Rio de Janeiro

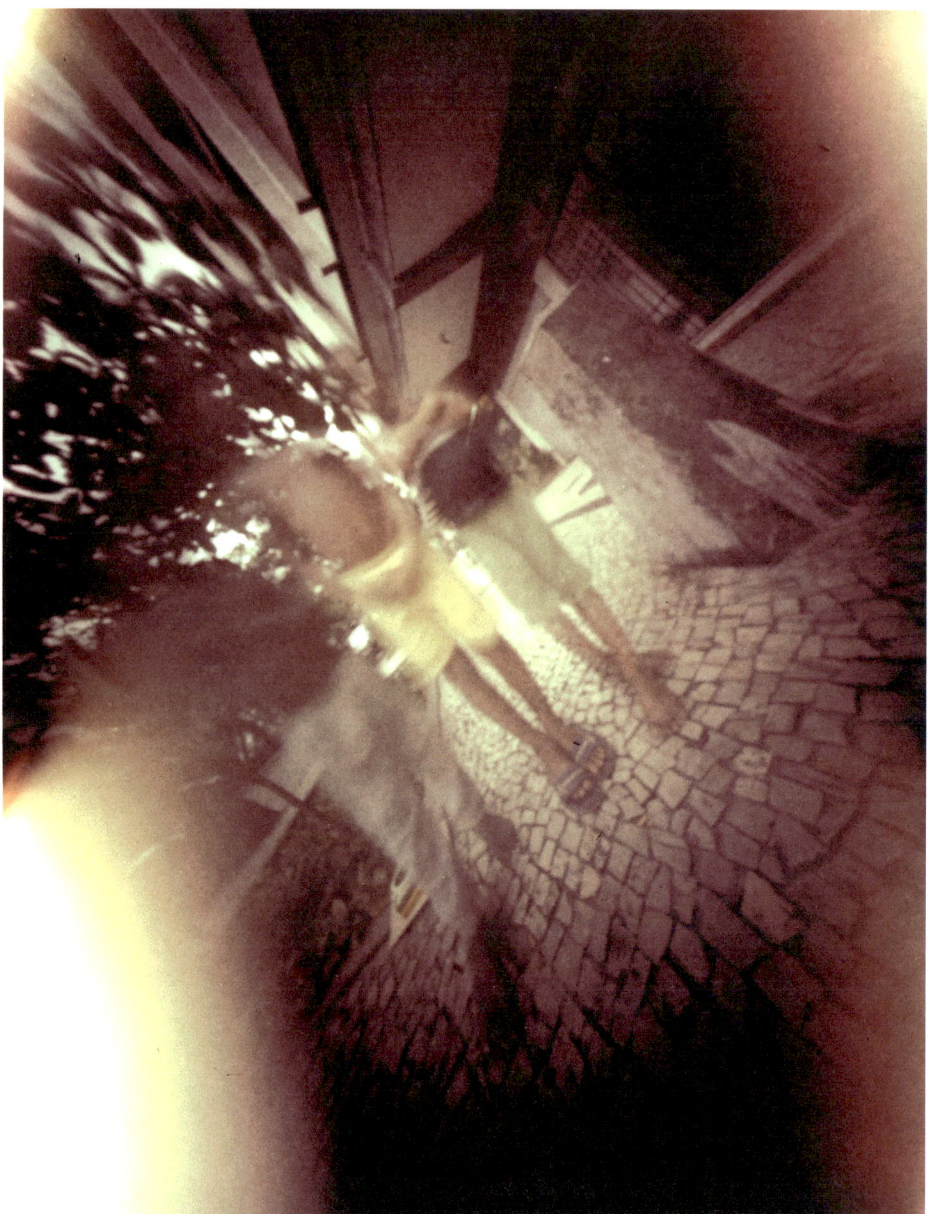

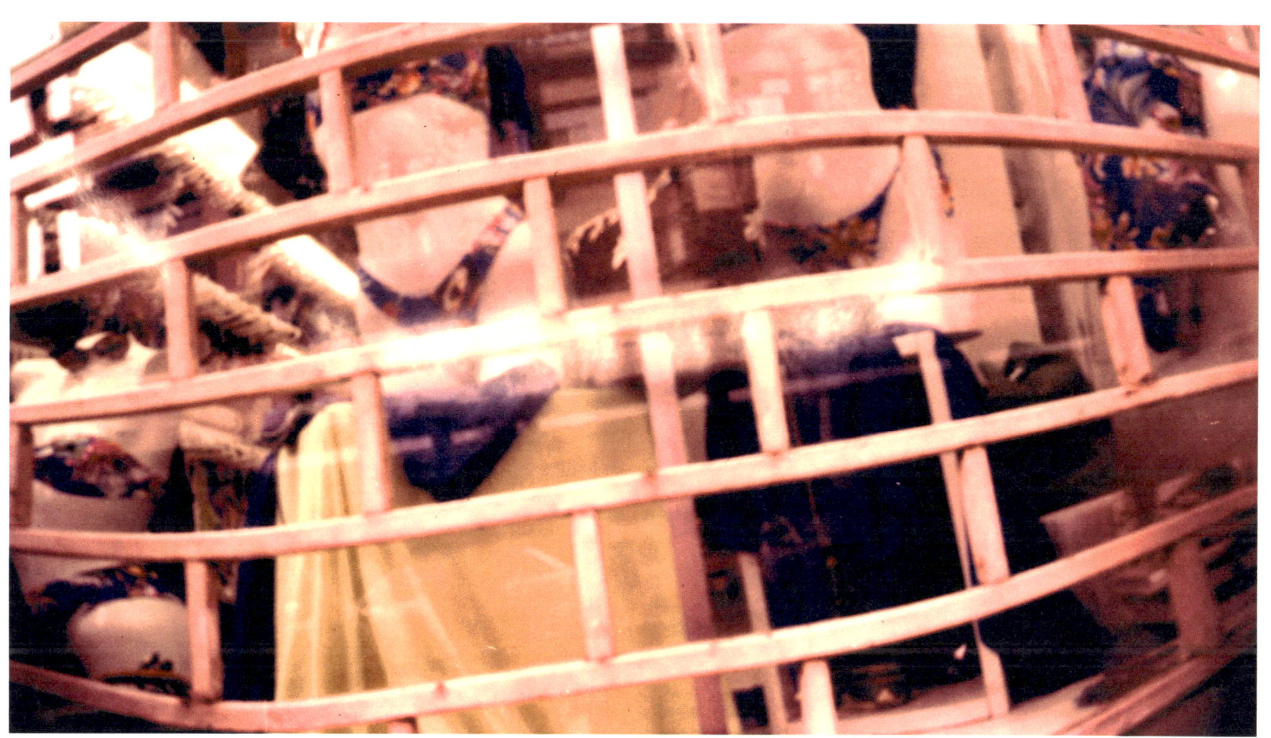

Paula Trope in collaboration with Xuxu,
Muller, Jero, and Fefei

Panel 1:
Xuxu, Muller, Jero, e Fefei
53.5 x 42.3 ins.

Panel 2:
Sem título (A bola)
(*Untitled [The Ball]*)
16.3 x 38 ins.

From the series *Os Meninos* (*The Boys*), 1993–94
Pinhole camera photography on colored resin paper
Courtesy of Galeria Vermelho, São Paulo

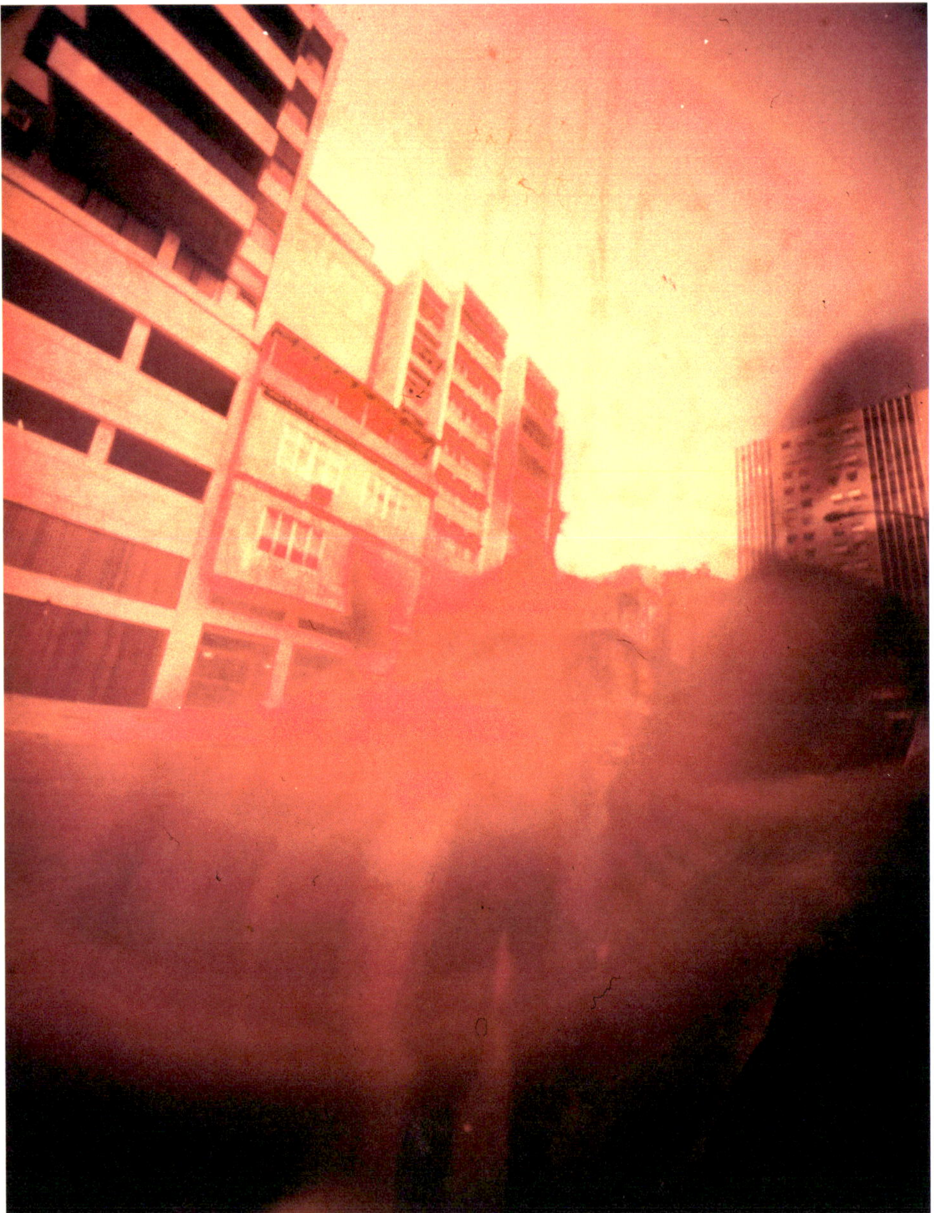

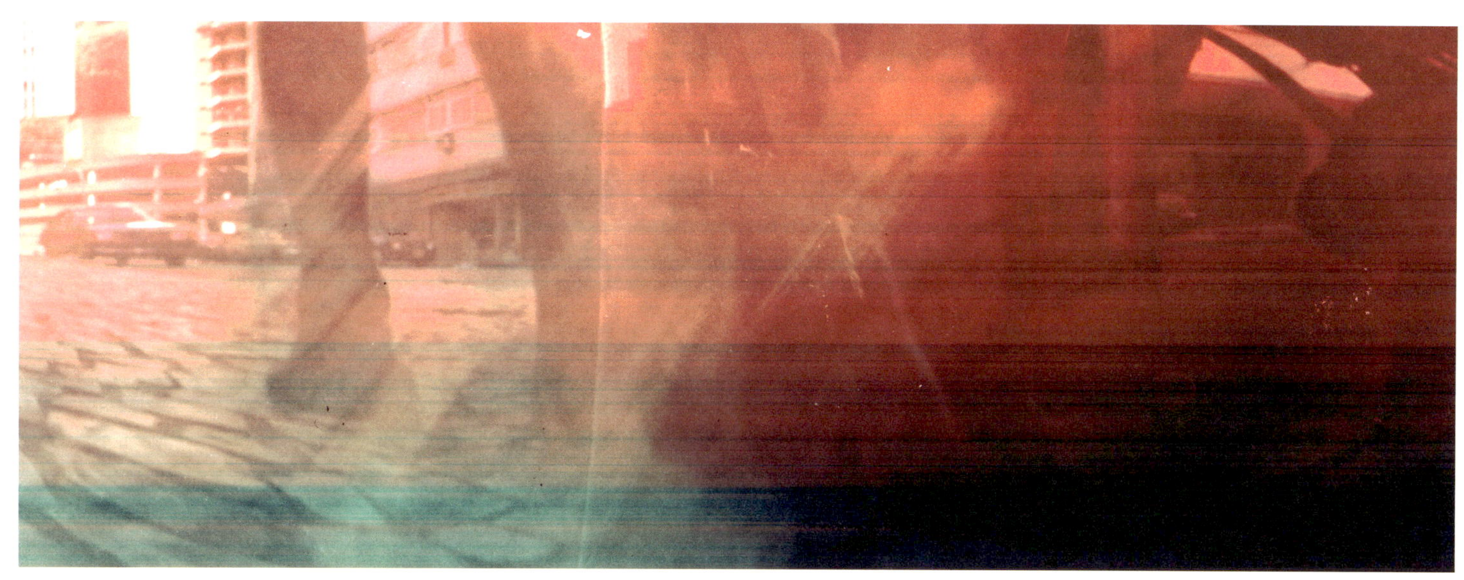

Paula Trope in collaboration with Jeferson and Nem

Panel 1:
Jeferson e Nem
64 x 42.3 ins.

Panel 2:
Sem título (A águia)
(*Untitled [The Eagle]*)
20.3 x 20.3 ins.

From the series *Os Meninos* (*The Boys*), 1993–94
Pinhole camera photography on colored resin paper
Collection of Paulo Roberto Santi, Rio de Janeiro

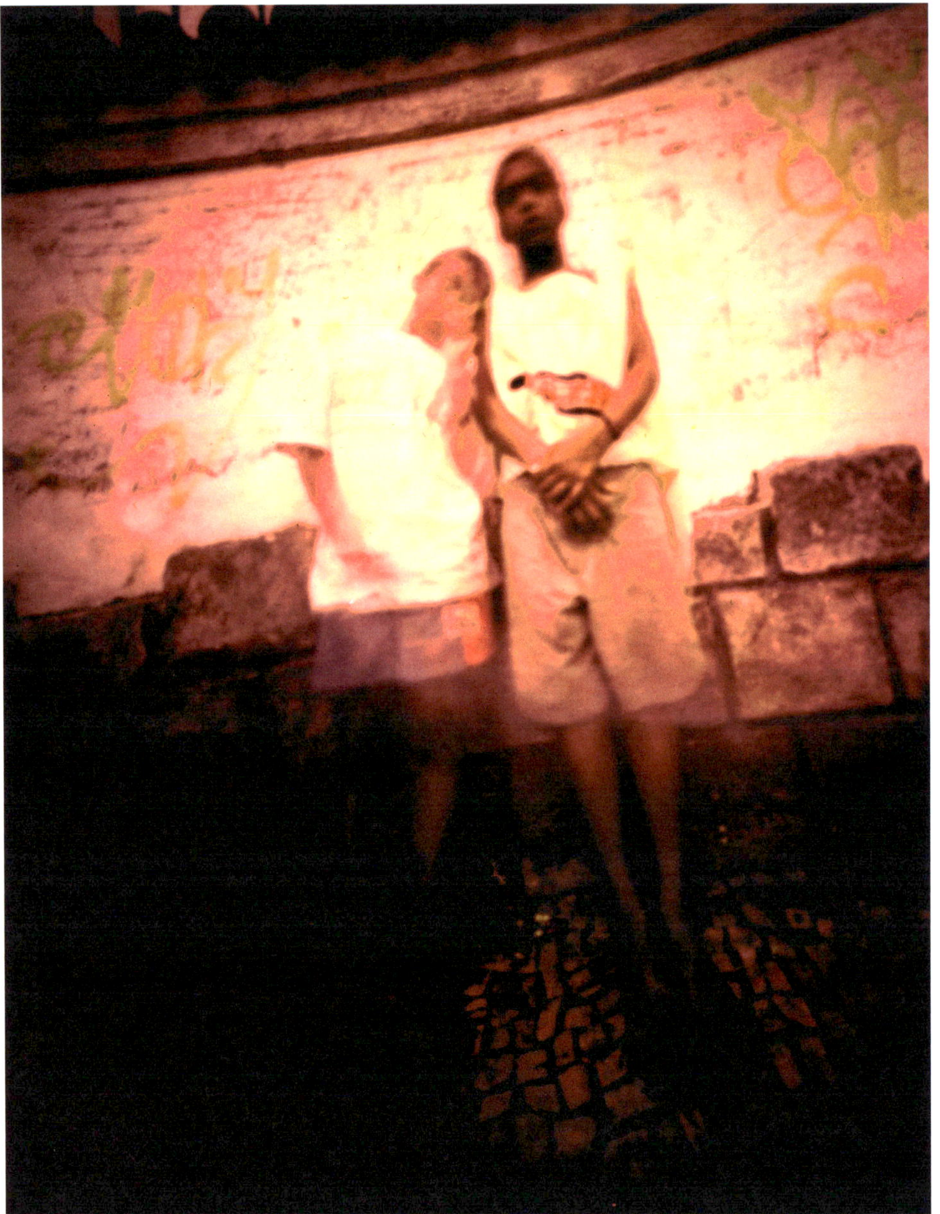

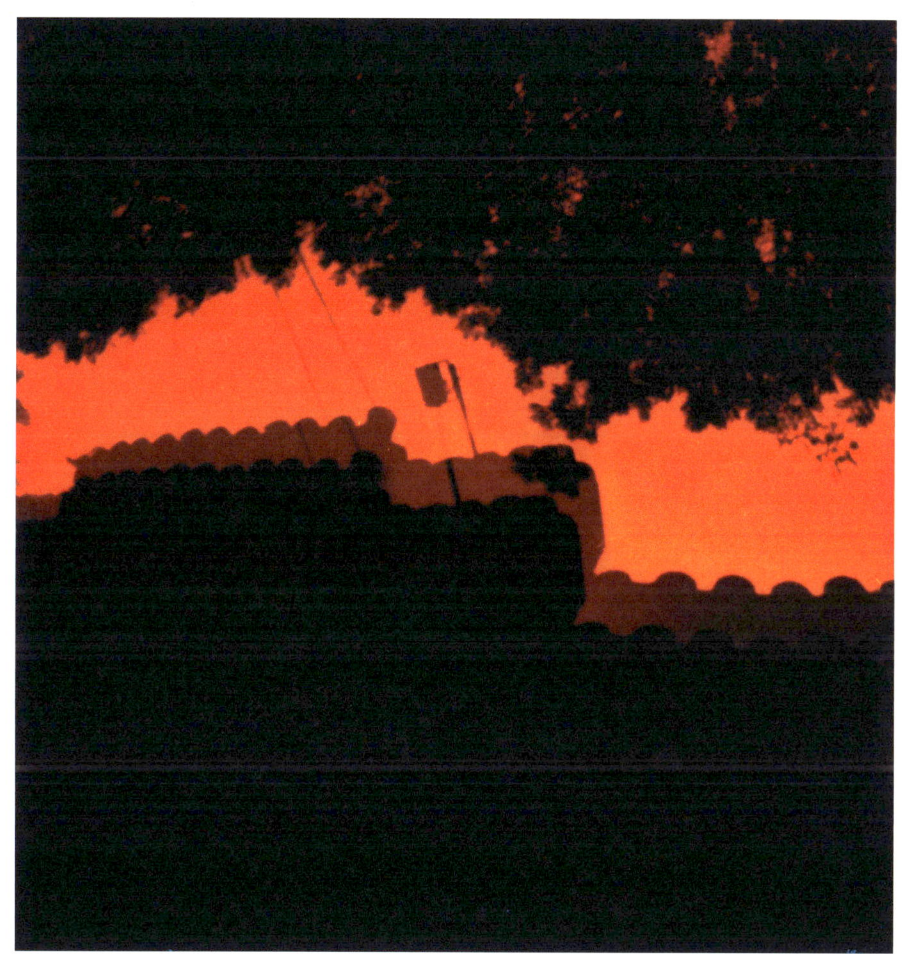

Paula Trope in collaboration with Bolinha

Panel 1:
Bolinha, aos 15
(*Bolinha, 15 years old*)
91.7 x 52.3 ins.

Panel 2:
Sem título (Bolinha ficou com a câmera)
(*Untitled [Bolinha kept the camera]*)
24.2 x 24.2 ins.

From the series *Os Meninos* (*The Boys*), 1993–94
Pinhole camera photography on colored resin paper
Coleção Gilberto Chateaubriand,
Museu de Arte Moderna, Rio de Janeiro

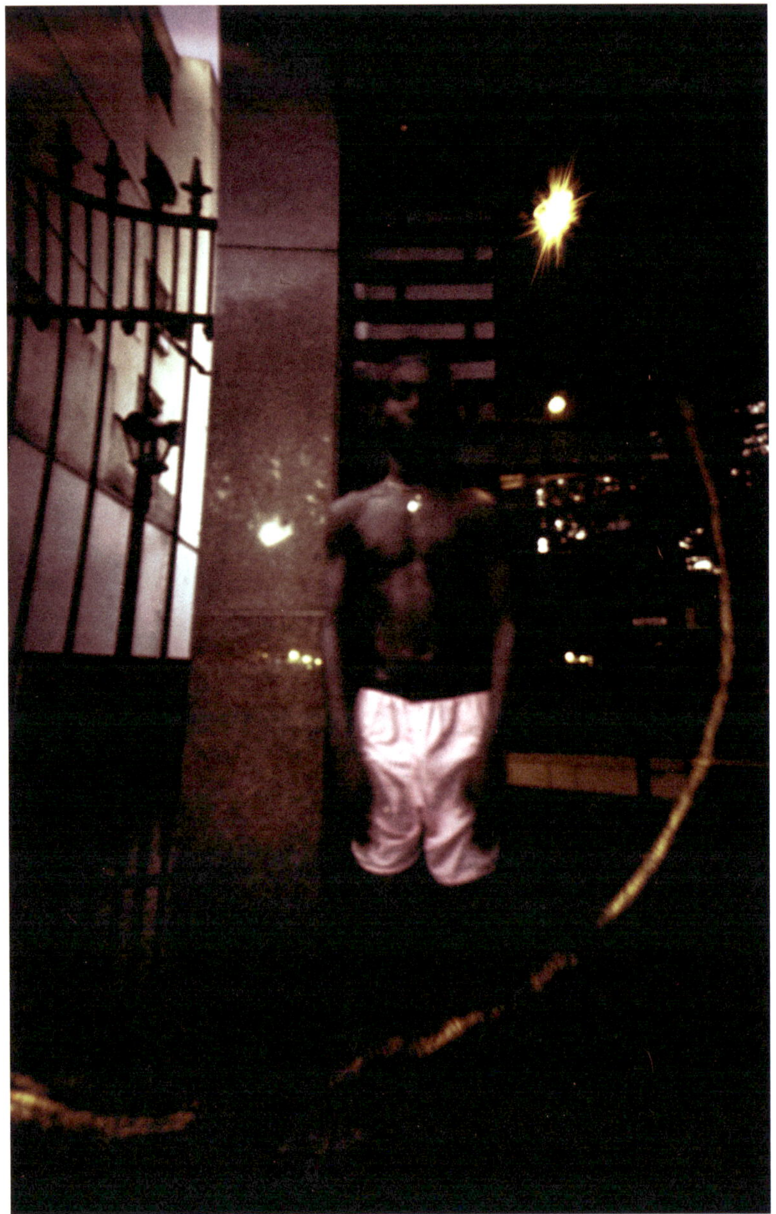

Paula Trope in collaboration with
Rodrigo de Maceda Perpétuo

Panel 1:
Rodrigo de Maceda Perpétuo, aos 20 anos
(*Rodrigo de Maceda Perpétuo, 20 years old*)
70.8 x 57.4 ins.

Panel 2:
TPC–"Tudo Pelo Certo." Parte alta do Querosene,
Terceiro Comando, Morrinho (*All for Doing the*
Right Thing. The High Side of Querosene Hill,
Terceiro Comando, Morrinho)
18.5 x 50.3 ins.

Panel 3:
Visão da boca e do PJL–"Paz, Justiça, e Liber-
dade," Morro do Fogueteiro, Santa Teresa,
Morrinho (*View of a Drug-Dealing Location*
and the PJL–"Peace, Justice, Freedom,"
Fogueteiro Hill, Santa Teresa, Morrinho)
20 x 50.7 ins.

Triptych from the series *Sem Simpatia*
(*Without Sympathy*), 2004–5
Pinhole camera photography on colored resin paper
Courtesy of Galeria Vermelho, São Paulo

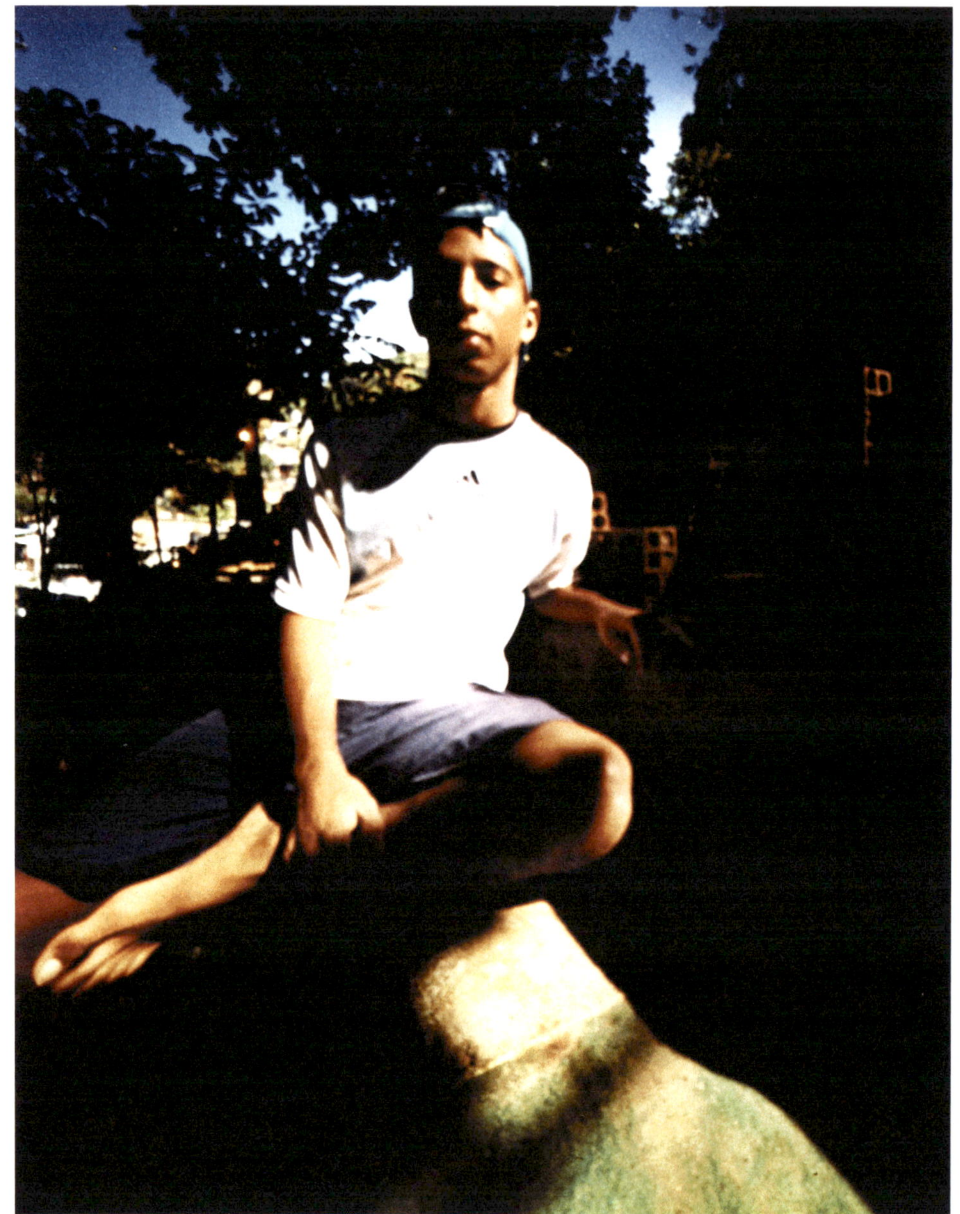

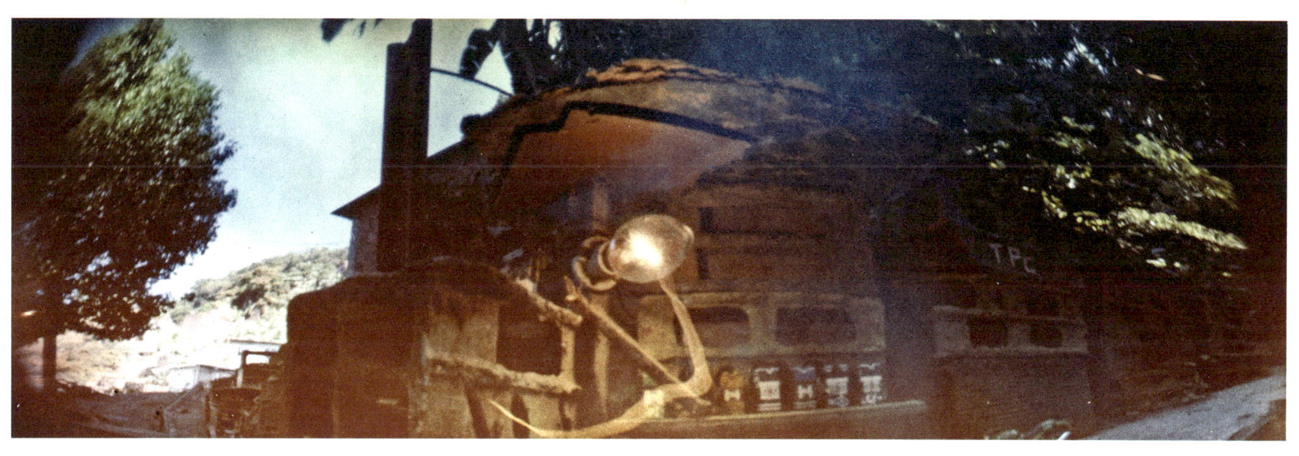

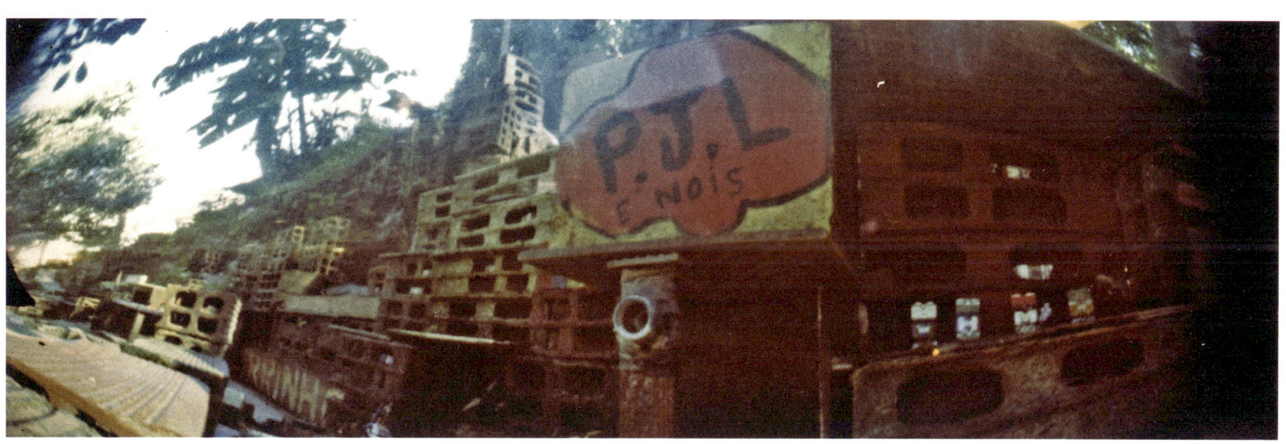
P.J.L
É NOIS

Paula Trope in collaboration with Marcos
Vinicius Clemente Ferreira (Negão)

Panel 1:
*Marcos Vinicius Clemente Ferreira (Negão),
aos 16* (*Marcos Vinicius Clemente Ferreira
[Negão], 16 years old*)
70.8 x 57.4 ins.

Panel 2:
*Começo do Baile, Morro do Salgueiro,
Morrinho* (*The Funk Dance Begins, Salgueiro
Hill, Morrinho*)
20 x 51.9 ins.

From the series *Sem Simpatia*
(*Without Sympathy*), 2004–5
Pinhole camera photography on colored resin paper
Coleção Gilberto Chateaubriand,
Museu de Arte Moderna, Rio de Janeiro

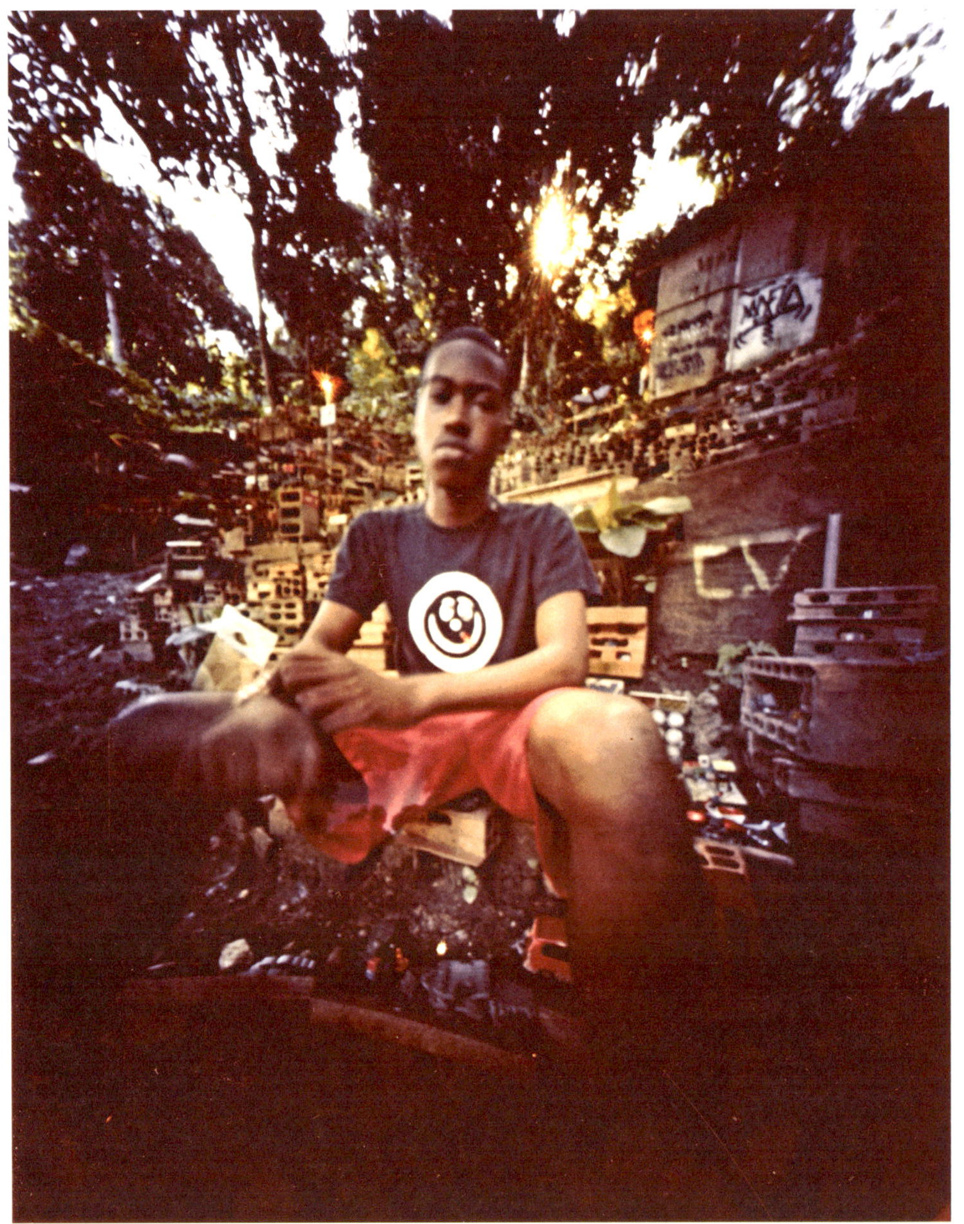

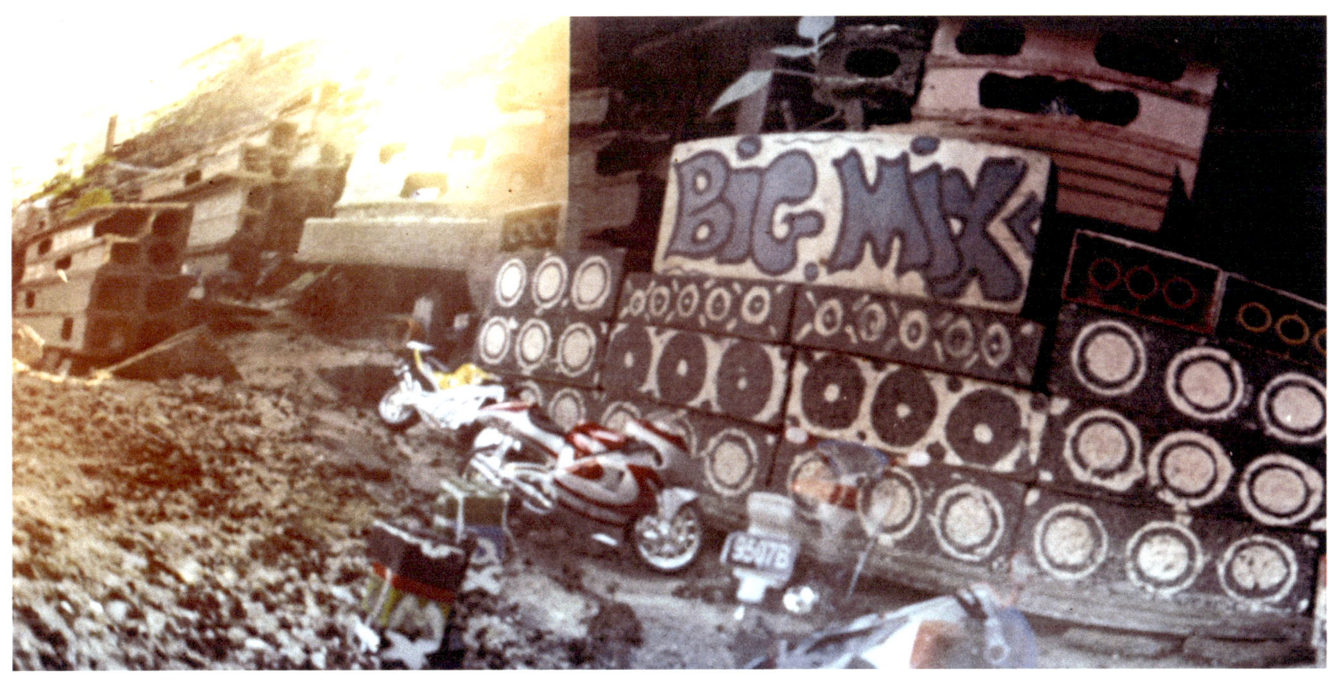
BIG.MIX

Paula Trope in collaboration
with Leandro de Paiva Adriano (Lê)

Panel 1:
Leandro de Paiva Adriano (Lê), aos 17
(*Leandro de Paiva Adriano [Lê], 17 years old*)
70.8 x 57.4 ins.

Panel 2:
Estátua do Complexo do Alemão, Morrinho
(*Statue at the Alemão Complex, Morrinho*)
20.8 x 51.1 ins.

From the series *Sem Simpatia*
(*Without Sympathy*), 2004–5
Pinhole camera photography on colored resin paper
Collection of the artist, Rio de Janeiro

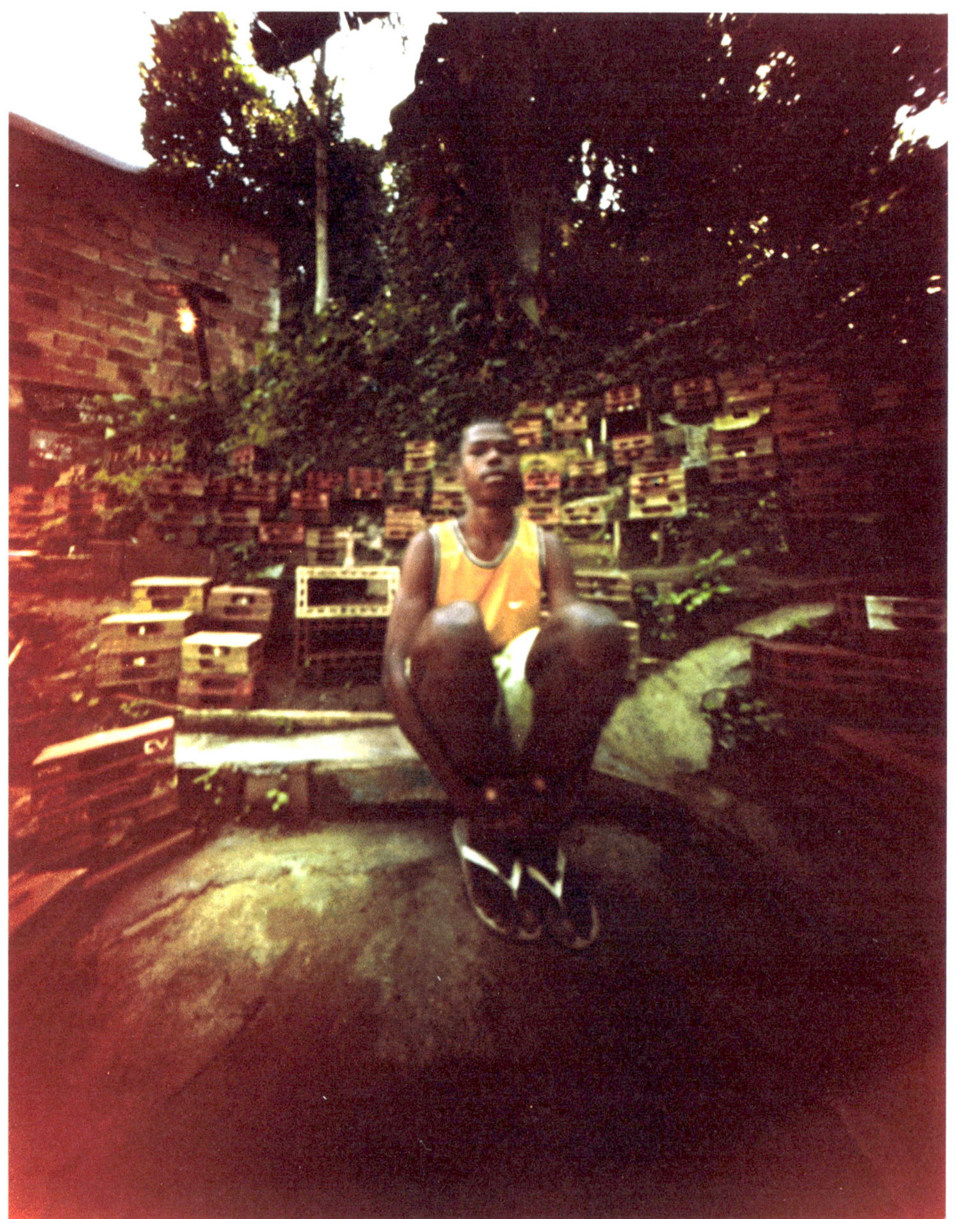

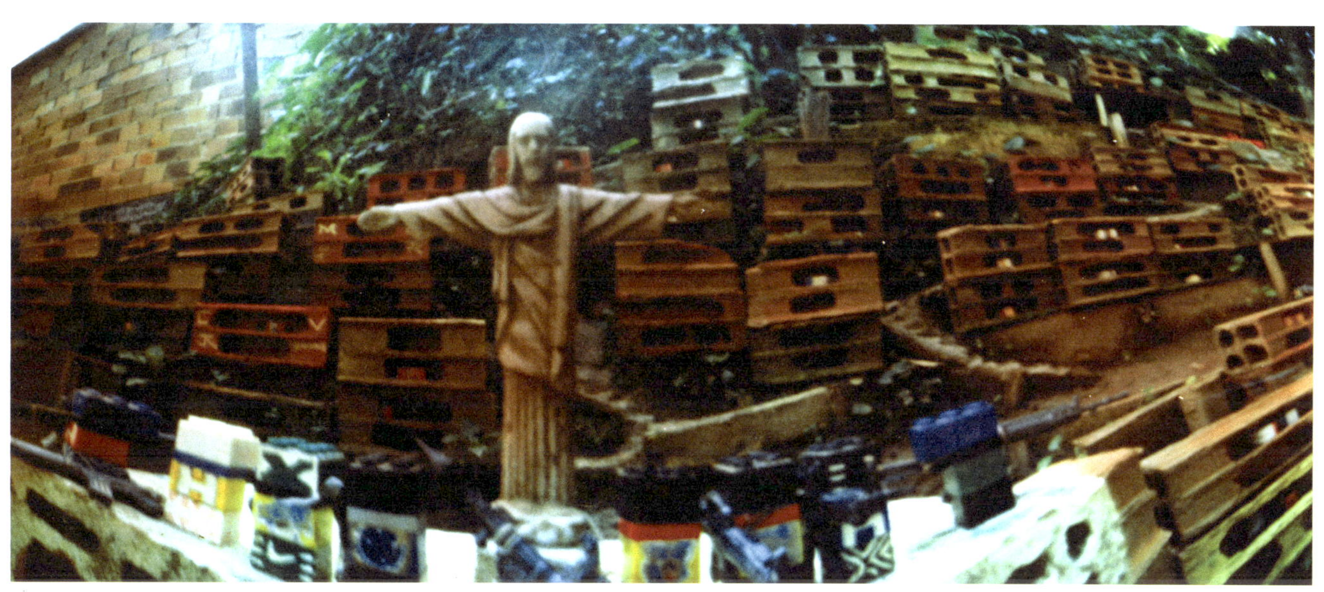

Paula Trope in collaboration with Renato Dias
Figueiredo (Naldão), Marcos Vinicius Clemente
Ferreira (Negão), Luciano de Alemeida, and
José Carlos da Silva Pereira (Júnior)

Panel 1:
Renato Dias Figueiredo (Naldão),
Marcos Vinicius Clemente Ferreira (Negão),
Luciano de Almeida, e José Carlos da Silva
Pereira (Júnior), aos 22, 16, 18 e 21 anos
(*Renato Dias Figueiredo [Naldão],*
Marcos Vinicius Clemente Ferreira [Negão],
Luciano de Almeida, and José Carlos da Silva
Pereira [Júnior], 22, 16, 18, and 21 years old)
70.8 x 57.4 ins.

Panel 2:
Bandidos do Borel e da Formiga na reunião!
Morrinho (*Outlaws of Borel and Formiga at a*
Meeting! Morrinho)
19.6 x 47.6 ins.

Panel 3:
Reunião no Morro do Salgueiro, Morrinho
(*Meeting at Salgueiro Hill, Morrinho*)
22.4 x 42.5 ins.

Panel 4:
Carro, Morro do Turano, Morrinho
(*Car, Turano Hill, Morrinho*)
20.4 x 46 ins.

Panel 5:
Os Braços, Morro dos Prazeres, Morrinho
(*Homeboys, Prazeres Hill, Morrinho*)
19.2 x 48 ins.

From the series *Sem Simpatia*
(*Without Sympathy*), 2004–5
Pinhole camera photography on colored resin paper
Courtesy of Galeria Vermelho, São Paulo

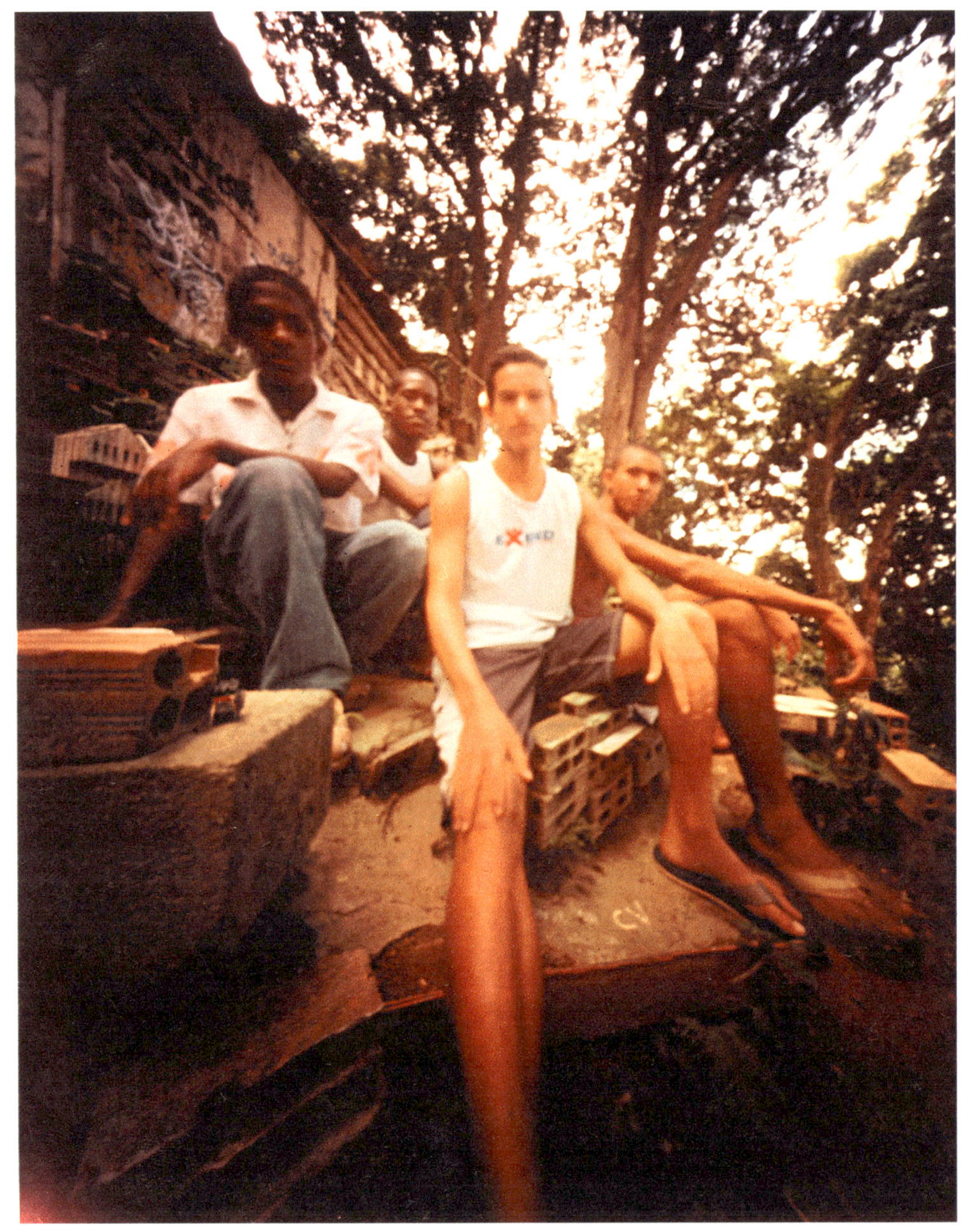

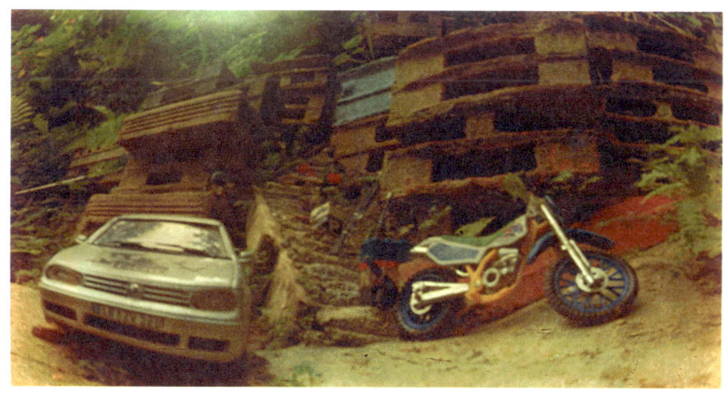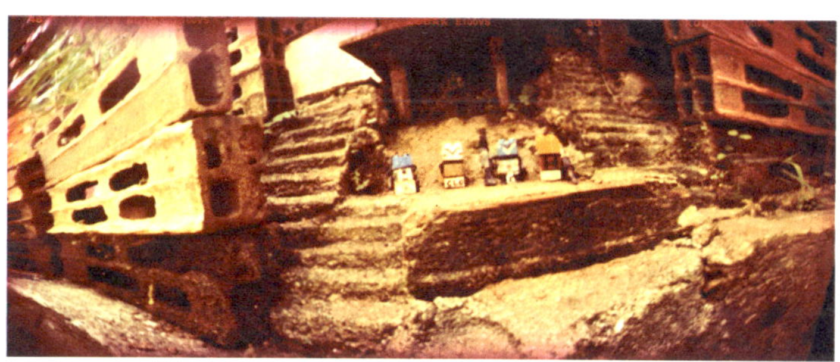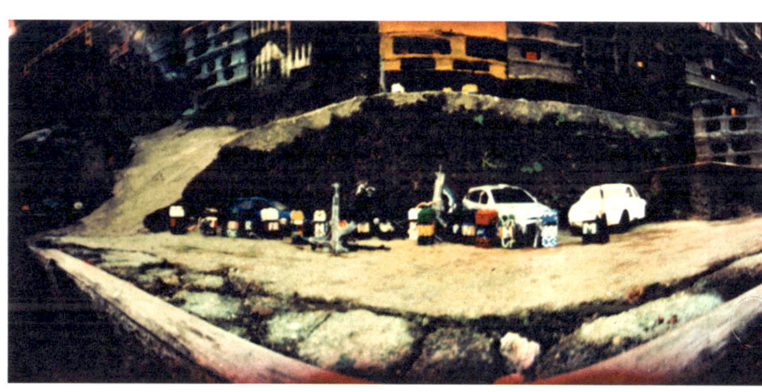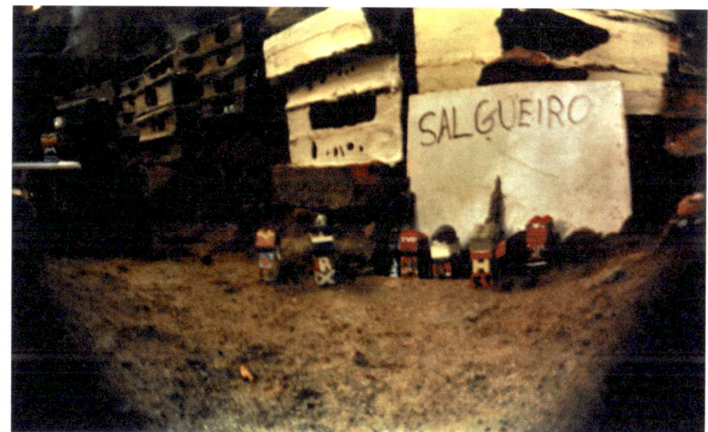
SALGUEIRO

Paula Trope in collaboration
with Nelcirlan Souza de Oliveira (Beiço) and
Maycon Souza de Oliveira (Maiquinho)

Panel 1:
*Nelcirlan (Beiço) e Maycon (Maiquinho) Souza
de Oliveira, aos 22 e 15* (*Nelcirlan [Beiço] and
Maycon [Maiquinho] Souza de Oliveira, 22
and 15 years old*)
70 x 56.2 ins.

Panel 2:
*Vida loka da comunidade, Fogueteiro Hill,
Morrinho* (*Crazy Life of the Community,
Fogueteiro Hill, Morrinho*)
20 x 49.6 ins.

Panel 3:
*Conversa entre traficantes, Morro do Andaraí,
Morrinho* (*Dealers in Conversation, Andaraí
Hill, Morrinho*)
58 x 22.8 ins.

From the series *Sem Simpatia* (*Without Sympathy*), 2004–5
Pinhole camera photography on colored resin paper
Collection of the artist, Rio de Janeiro

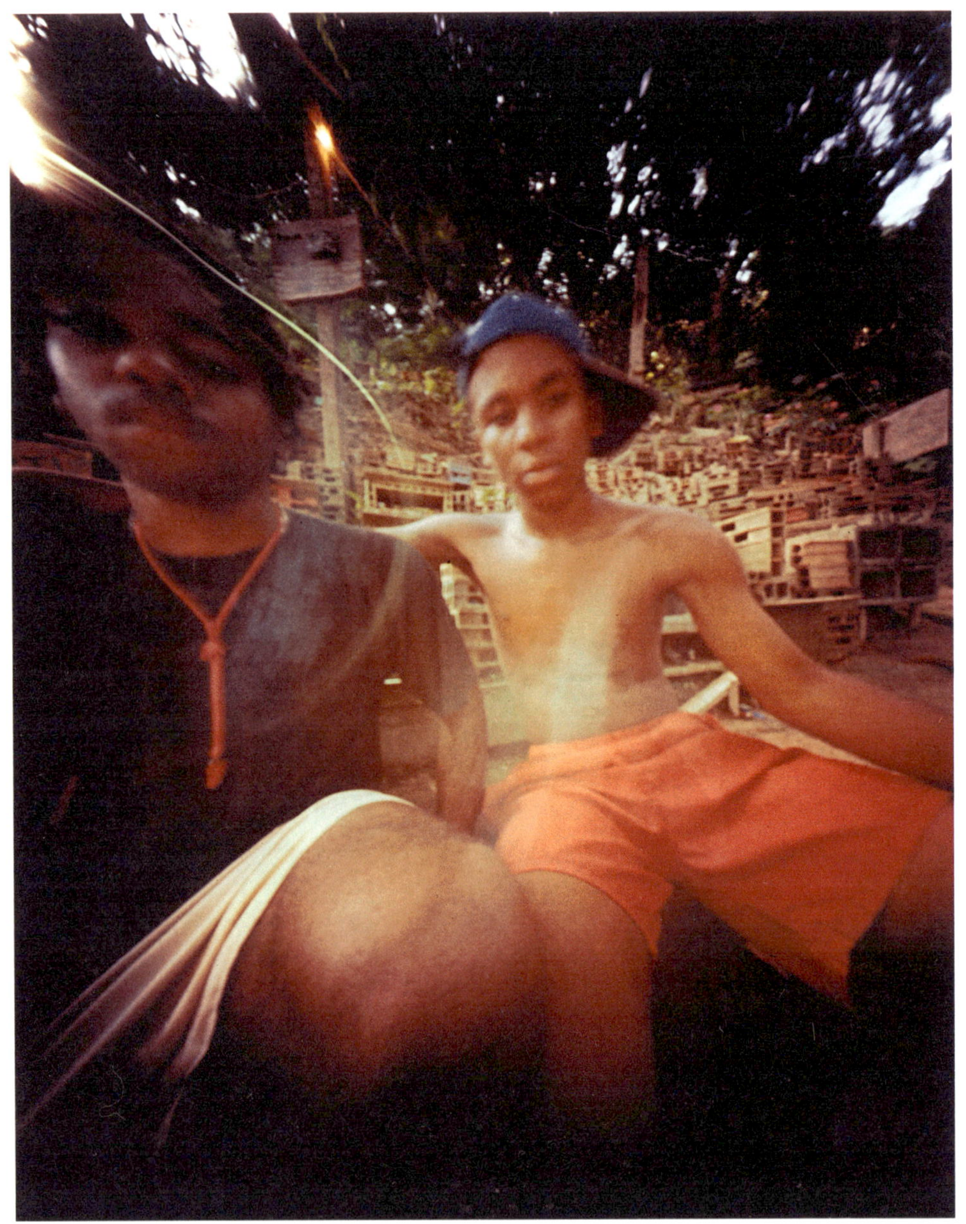

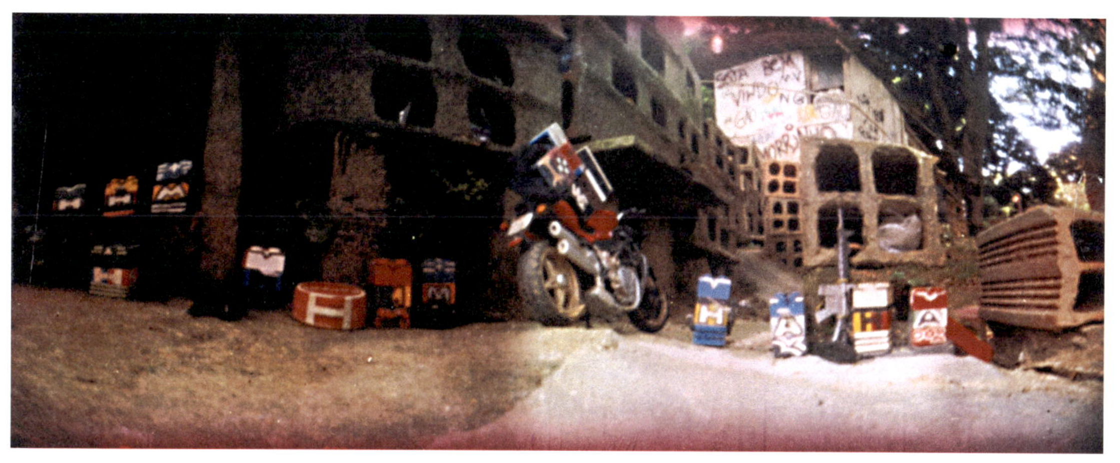

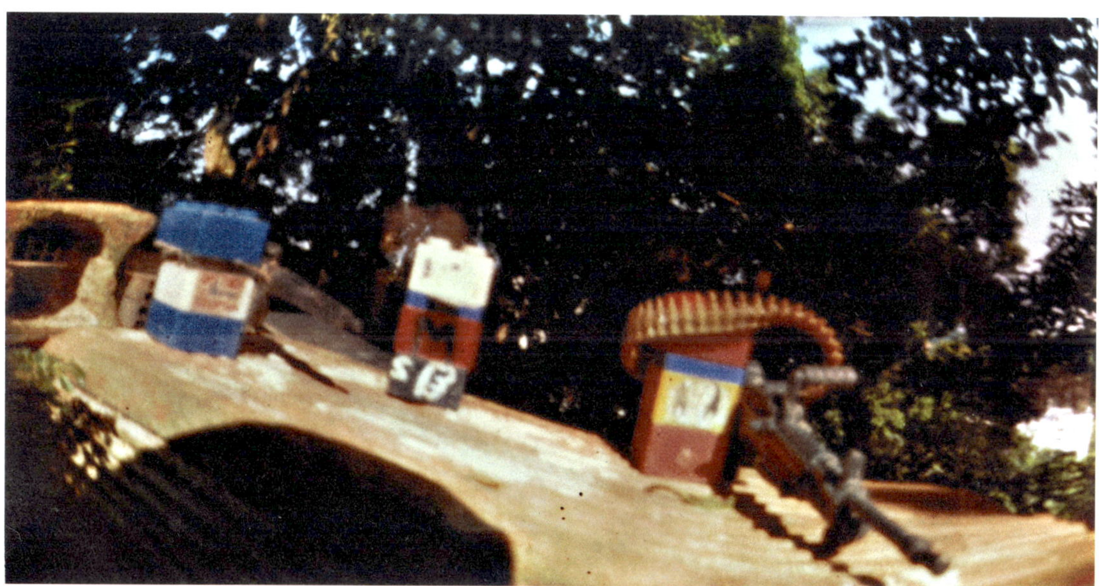

Paula Trope
Contos de Passagem (*Passage Tales*), 2001

Video series in progress
Pinhole video
22 minutes, looped
Collection of the artist, Rio de Janeiro

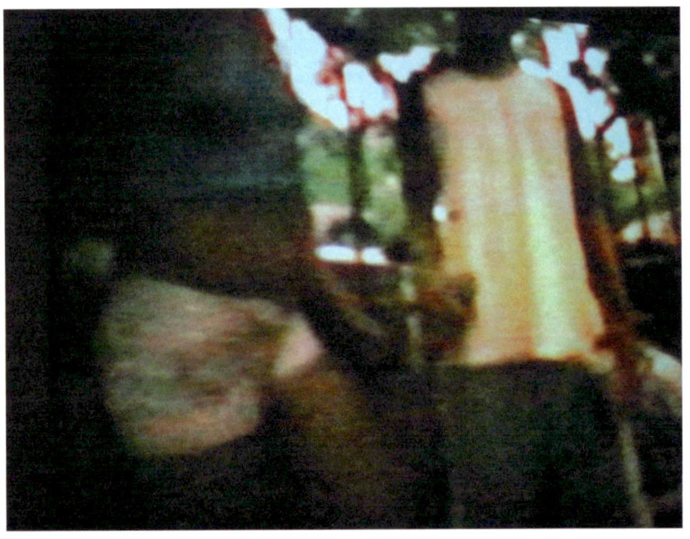

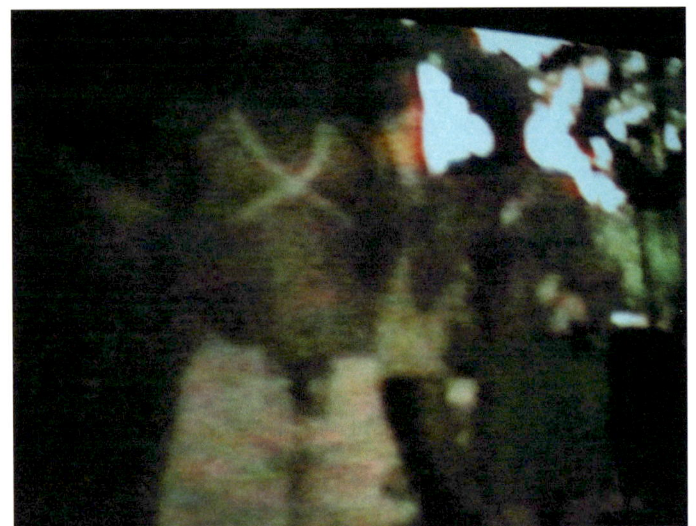

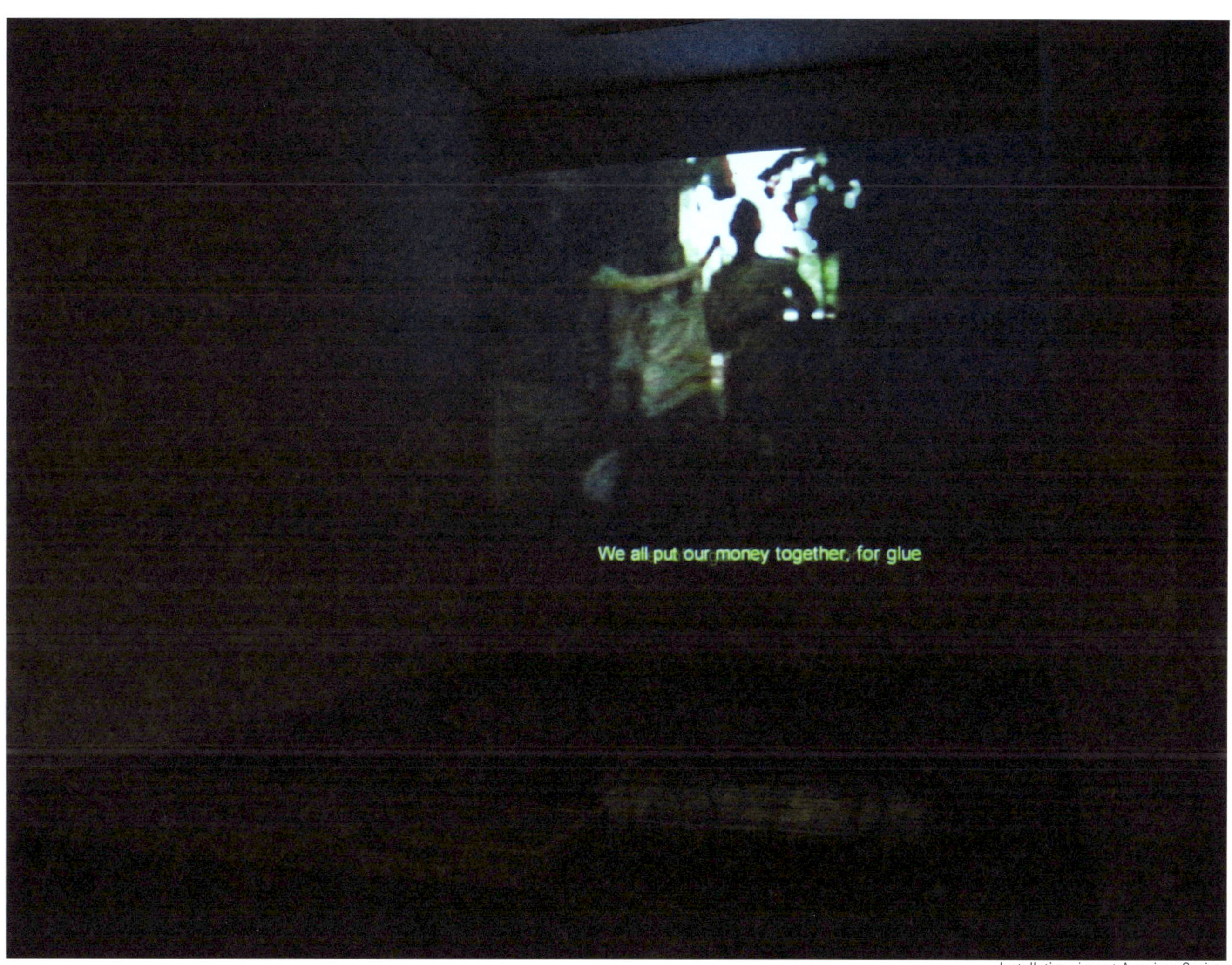

Installation view at Americas Society

Installation view of Paula Trope's *Traslados*
(*On the Move*), 1996–98
Slide installation at the Americas Society Art Gallery, 2007
Photographs by Arturo Sánchez

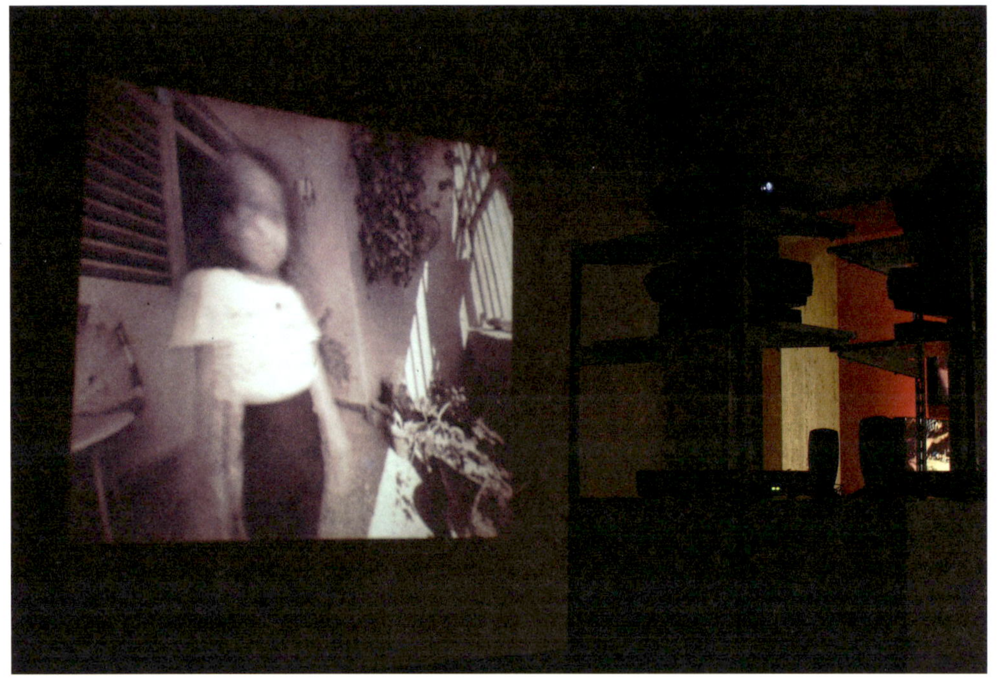

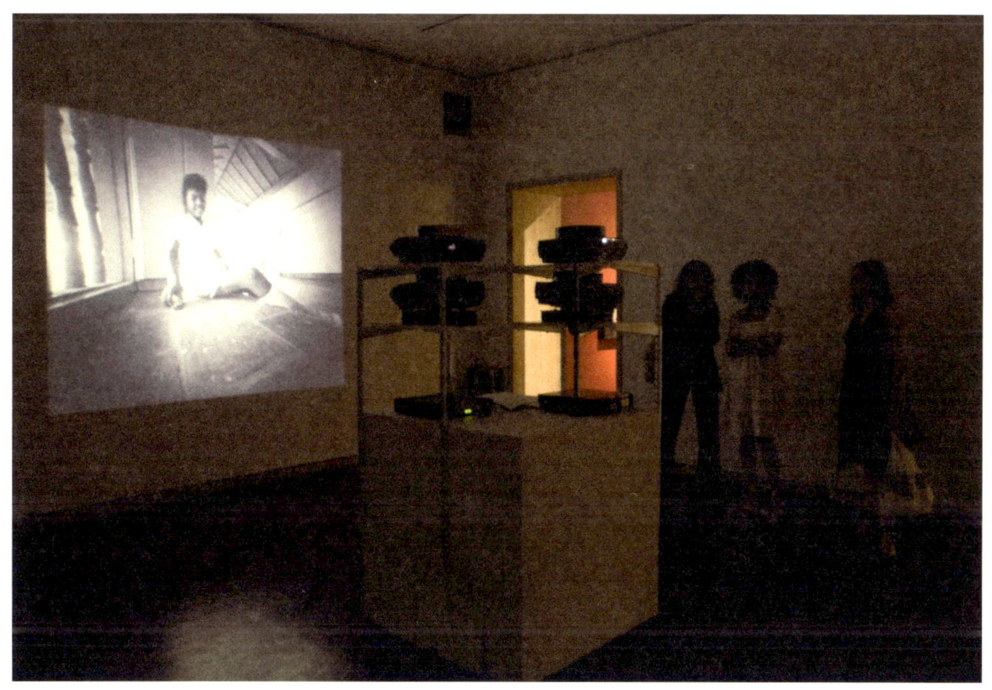

Paula Trope
Slides from *Traslados* (*On the Move*),
1996–98
Slide installation
Collection of the artist, Rio de Janeiro

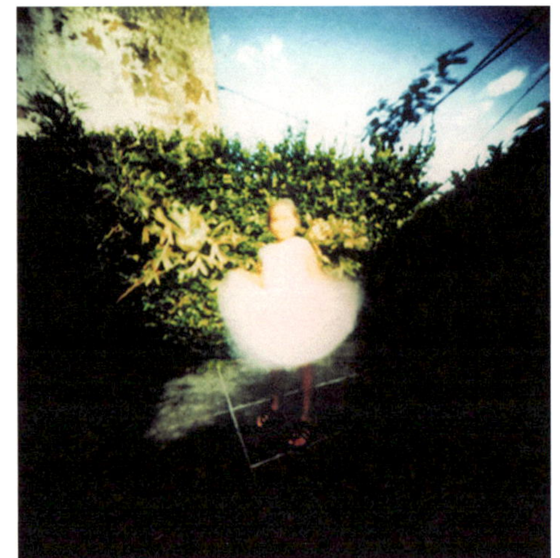

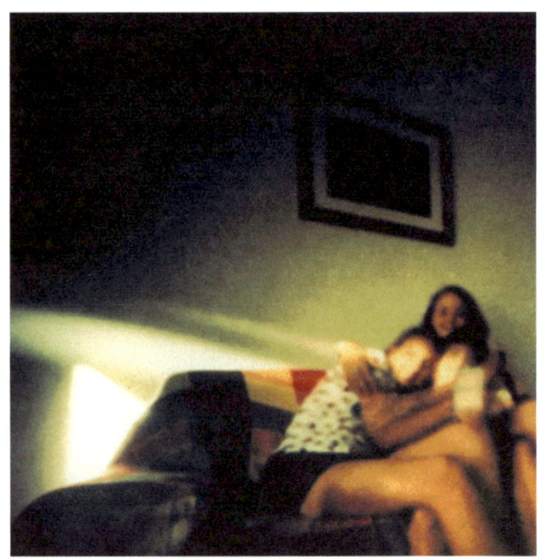

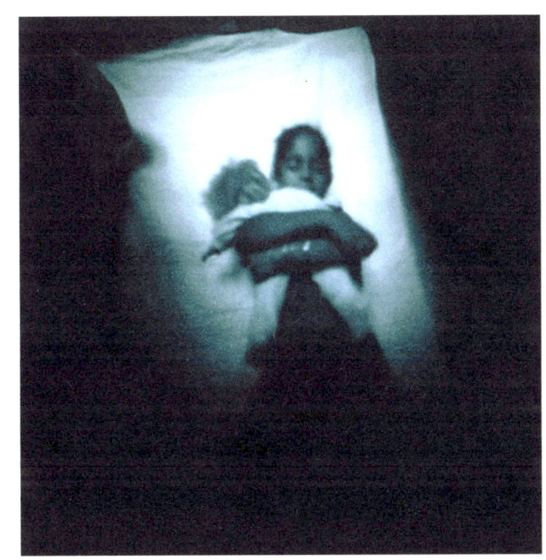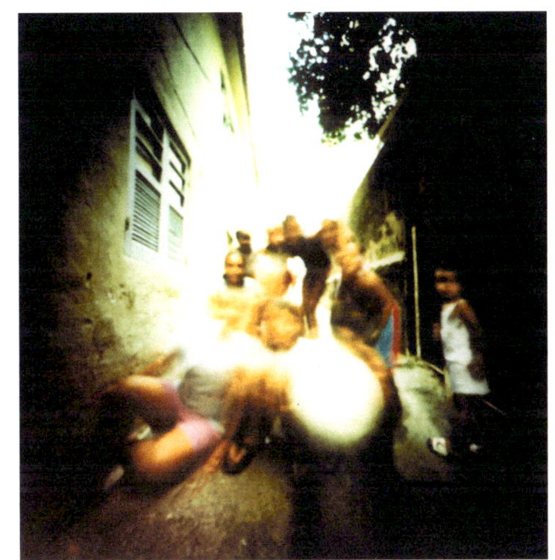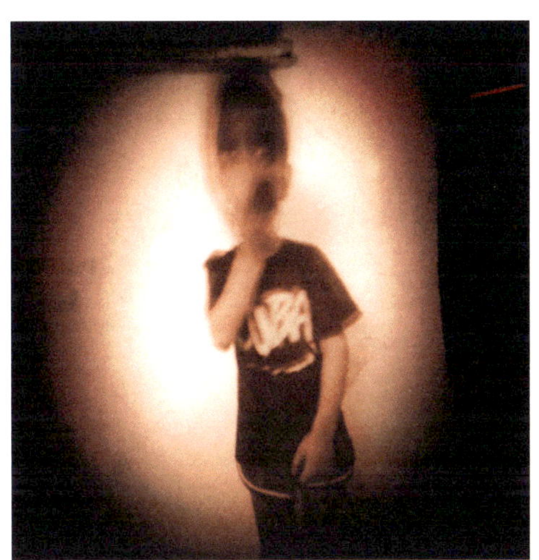

PAULA TROPE
B. RIO DE JANEIRO, 1962

Education:

1995–99
M.S., Techniques and Poetics of Image and Sound
School of Arts and Communication, Universidade
de São Paulo, Brazil

1985–89
B.A., Social Communications, Cinema
Institute of the Arts and Social Communications,
Universidade Federal Fluminense, Niterói, Brazil

Research:

1993
Traces (with Sophie Calle)
International Center of Photography,
New York, USA

1989–91
Research on personal language in photography
(with Eduardo Brandão)
Escola de Artes Visuais, Parque Lage,
Rio de Janeiro, Brazil

Selected Solo Exhibitions:

2010
Exílios
Casa de Cultura da UEL, Londrina, Brazil

2007
**Emancipatory Action: Paula Trope and
the Meninos**
Americas Society, New York, USA

2006
Exílios
Muzeum Sztuki Nowoczesnej w Warszawie, as part
of the Polonia Carioca Festival, Warsaw, Poland

2003
Contos de Passagem
Pilot Project, Espaço Cultural Sérgio Porto,
Rio de Janeiro, Brazil

1998
Traslados
Paço das Artes, São Paulo; Pandora X;
Centro Cultural São Paulo, Brazil

1997
Instalation
Paço Imperial, Rio de Janeiro, Brazil

1996
Projeto '96
Galeria Camargo Vilaça, São Paulo, Brazil

1993
Os Meninos
Galeria Macunaíma, Funarte/IBAC,
Rio de Janeiro, Brazil

1992
Amor
Sala Imagem Gráfica, Escola de Artes Visuais,
Parque Lage, Rio de Janeiro; Sala Cândido Portinari,
Universidade do Estado do Rio de Janeiro, Brazil

Selected Group Exhibitions:

2010
**Novas Aquisições 2007–2010:
Coleção Gilberto Chateaubriand**
Museu de Arte Moderna, Rio de Janeiro, Brazil

2009
**LIVING TOGETHER:
Estrategias para la convivencia**
Centro Cultural Montehermoso Kulturunea,
Vitoria-Gasteiz, Spain

Fotografia: memória e arte
Casa do Saber, Rio de Janeiro, Brazil

2008
MAM 60 – FEBEARio
Espaço Cultural Sérgio Porto, Rio de Janeiro, Brazil

Extraña
Durex Arte Contemporânea, Rio de Janeiro, Brazil

2007
52. Biennale di Venezia
Arsenale, Venice, Italy

2006–7
**Desidentidade: Arte Brasileira Contemporânea
no Acervo do MAM**
Instituto Valenciano de Arte Moderno-IVAM,
Valencia, Spain

2006
27ª Bienal de São Paulo
Fundação Bienal de São Paulo, Brazil

Arte Pará 2006
Fundação Rômulo Maiorana, Pará, Brazil

Manobras Radicais
Centro Cultural do Banco do Brasil, São Paulo, Brazil

**Sem Título 2006: Comodato Eduardo Brandão
e Jan Fjeld**
Museu de Arte Moderna, São Paulo, Brazil

Onde: O Lugar na poética contemporânea
Galeria LGC Arte Contemporânea,
Rio de Janeiro, Brazil

2005–6
**Prêmio CNI-SESI Marcantonio Vilaça para
Artes Plásticas**
Museu de Arte Moderna Aloisto Magalhães-
MAMAM, Recife; Casa das 11 Janelas, Belém;
Santander Cultural, Porto Alegre; Museu Nacional
de Belas Artes, Rio de Janeiro; Instituto Tomie
Ohtake, São Paulo; Sede CNI, Rio de Janeiro, Brazil

2005
Além da Imagem
Centro Cultural Telemar, Rio de Janeiro, Brazil

Arte Pará 2005
Fundação Rômulo Maiorana, Pará, Brazil

**10 Anos de um Novo MAM: Antologia
do Acervo**
Museu de Arte Moderna, São Paulo, Brazil

Viés
Galeria Vermelho, São Paulo, Brazil

Mostra Corpo Câmera Ação
Instituto Cultural Itaú, São Paulo, Brazil

O Retrato como Imagem do Mundo
Museu de Arte Moderna, São Paulo, Brazil

O Corpo na Arte Contemporânea Brasileira
Instituto Cultural Itaú, São Paulo, Brazil

Chroma
Museu de Arte Moderna, Rio de Janeiro, Brazil

2004–5
Coleções IV
Galeria Mercedes Viegas, Rio de Janeiro, Brazil

Olho Vivo: A Arte da Fotografia
Santander Cultural, Porto Alegre, Brazil

2004

Arte Pará 2004
Fundação Rômulo Maiorana, Belém, Brazil

Paralela
São Paulo, Brazil

Espaço Lúdico: Um Olhar sobre a Infância na Arte Brasileira
Espaço BNDES, Rio de Janeiro, Brazil

2003–4

A Subversão dos Meios
Instituto Cultural Itaú, São Paulo, Brazil

2003

O Cinema na Fotografia Contemporânea
Galeria LGC Arte Hoje, Rio de Janeiro, Brazil

Meus Amigos
MAM Espaço Villa Lobos, São Paulo, Brazil

2002

Coleção de Fotografia do MAM
Museu de Arte Moderna, São Paulo, Brazil

Coletiva de inauguração
Galeria Vermelho, São Paulo, Brazil

2001

Versiones del Sur: Más Allá del Documento
Museo Nacional Centro de Arte Reina Sofía, Madrid, Spain

Entre a Palabra e a Imagem
Museu de Arte Moderna, Rio de Janeiro, Brazil

2000

Novas Aquisições: Coleção Gilberto Chateaubriand
Museu de Arte Moderna, Rio de Janeiro, Brazil

1999

Panorama da Arte Brasileira
Museu de Arte Moderna, São Paulo; Museu de Arte Contemporânea de Niterói, Brazil

1997

El Indivíduo y Su Memoria
6ª Bienal de La Habana, Havana, Cuba

Identidade/ Não Identidade
Museu de Arte Moderna, São Paulo; Centro Cultural Light, Rio de Janeiro, Brazil

1996

Limites da Fotografía
SESC Pompéia, São Paulo, Brazil

1995

Panorama da Arte Brasileira
Museu de Arte Moderna, São Paulo; Museu de Arte Moderna, Rio de Janeiro, Brazil

1994

A Espessura da Luz: Fotografia Brasileira Contemporânea
Fotografie Forum, Frankfurt, Germany

Mix Brasil: Outros Territórios
Museu da Imagem e do Som, São Paulo, Brazil

Encuentro Interamericano de Artistas Plásticos
Palácio das Artes, Guadalajara, Mexico

1993

17º Salão Carioca de Arte
RioArte, Rio de Janeiro, Brazil

Na Falta da Verdade
Casa Triângulo, São Paulo, Brazil

Paixão do Olhar
Museu de Arte Moderna, Rio de Janeiro, Brazil

Projeto Macunaíma
Funarte/IBAC, Rio de Janeiro, Brazil

1992
Identidade: Do Analógico ao Digital
Galeria de Arte UFF, Niterói, Brazil

**Brasilien Entdeckung und Selbstentdeckung
Das Brasilien Der Brasilianer**
Kunsthaus Zürich, Switzerland

1991
13 Fotógrafos X 13 Fotos
Galeria 110 Arte Contemporânea,
Rio de Janeiro, Brazil

1990
Iconógrafos: 16 Fotógrafos Hoje
Museu de Arte Moderna, São Paulo; Galeria da
EAV, Parque Lage, Rio de Janeiro, Brazil

1989
O Mestre á Mostra
Galeria EAV, Parque Lage, Rio de Janeiro, Brazil

1985
Circo de Imagens
Mezanino do Metrô Carioca, Secretaria Municipal
de Educação e Cultura, Rio de Janeiro, Brazil

1984
História Sem Choro Nem Vela
Cineclube Macunaíma–ABI, Rio de Janeiro, Brazil

1983
**Um Outro Cinema: A Aventura e o Desafio do
Cinema Minoritário**
Cinemateca do Museu de Arte Moderna,
Rio de Janeiro; Centro Cultural Calouste Gulbenkian,
Rio de Janeiro, Brazil

Awards:

2004
**Prêmio CNI-SESI Marcantonio Vilaça
para Artes Plásticas**
Rio de Janeiro, Brazil

1999
5º Programa de Bolsas RioArte
Instituto Municipal de Arte e Cultura,
Secretaria Municipal de Cultura;
Prefeitura da Cidade do Rio de Janeiro, Brazil

1995
Panorama da Arte Brasileira
Museu de Arte Moderna, São Paulo and
Museu de Arte Moderna, Rio de Janeiro,
Prêmio Estímulo PricewaterhouseCoopers, Brazil

Selected Collections:

Carlos Barrozo
Rio de Janeiro, Brazil

Eduardo Brandão e Jan Fjeld
São Paulo, Brazil

Miguel Chaia
São Paulo, Brazil

**Coleção Gilberto Chateaubriand,
Museu de Arte Moderna**
Rio de Janeiro, Brazil

Coleção de Fotografia do Museu de Arte Moderna
São Paulo, Brazil

Fondation Cartier pour l'Art Contemporain
Paris, France

Luis Eduardo Gama e Silva
Rio de Janeiro, Brazil

Alfred Herzog
São Paulo, Brazil

Ignacio and Valentina Oberto
Caracas, Venezuela

Joaquim Paiva
Brasília, Brazil

Myriam Salomon
Paris, France

Susana Steinbruch Collection
São Paulo, Brazil

COLLABORATORS IN SEM SIMPATIA

Nelcirlan Souza de Oliveira – aka Beiço
Born 12/17/1982

Maycon Souza de Oliveira – aka Maiquinho
Born 06/25/1989

José Carlos da Silva Pereira – aka Júnior
Born 01/26/1984

Luciano de Almeida
Born 12/30/1986

Rodrigo de Maceda Perpétuo
Born 09/24/1983

Paulo Vitor da Silva Dias – aka Tovi
Born 07/18/1986

Raniere Dias – aka Rani
Born 08/24/1983

Renato Dias Figueiredo – aka Naldão
Born 10/31/1982

Felipe de Souza Dias – aka Lepé
Born 07/21/1987

Marcos Vinicius Clemente Ferreira – aka Negão
Born 03/27/1988

David Lucio Terra de Araújo – aka Forma
Born 01/01/1991

Esteives Lúcio Terra de Araújo – aka Teibe
Born 11/24/1993

Gustavo José dos Santos – aka Djou
Born 12/14/1991

Leandro de Paiva Adriano – aka Lê
Born 08/26/1986

Leonardo de Paiva Adriano – aka Nem
Born 05/02/1990

Irla Silva dos Santos – aka Plin-Plin
Born 11/15/1990

Bruno Silva dos Santos
Born 10/08/1989

ABOUT THE CONTRIBUTORS

Ute Meta Bauer

Ute Meta Bauer is Associate Professor and Director of the Visual Arts Program at the Massachusetts Institute of Technology in Cambridge, having served as Professor of Theory, Practice, and Mediation of Contemporary Art at the Academy of Fine Arts in Vienna (1996–2006) and as Founding Director of the Office for Contemporary Art Norway in Oslo (2002–5). She was Artistic Director of the 3rd Berlin Biennial for Contemporary Art (2003–4) and Co-Curator of Documenta 11 (2000–2), where she worked alongside Artistic Director Okwui Enwezor. She curated *Architectures of Discourse* at the Fundació Antoni Tàpies in Barcelona (2001) and *First Story—Women Building/New Narratives for the 21st Century* for the 2001 European Cultural Capital, Porto. She has been the editor of several art periodicals, including *META* in Stuttgart, *case* in Barcelona and Porto, and *Verkstedt* in Oslo. She has held positions at a number of cultural institutions, including Chairwoman of the Art Advisory Board of the Goethe Institute and Member of the International Board of the Bauhaus Foundation in Dessau. Most recently, she was nominated to be a member of the Curatorial Advisory Team of the 3rd Yokohama Triennial, 2008.

Paulo Herkenhoff

Paulo Herkenhoff is an independent curator and critic. He is the former director of the Museu Nacional de Belas Artes do Rio de Janeiro and has worked for a number of private collections and museums, including the Foundation Eva Klabin Rapaport in Rio de Janeiro and the Patricia Phelps de Cisneros Collection in Caracas. In addition, he has served as an Adjunct Curator in Painting and Sculpture at the Museum of Modern Art, New York; Artistic Director of the XXIV São Paulo Biennial (1997–99); and Curator of the Brazilian Pavilion at the 47th Venice Biennale (1997). Recent curatorial projects include *Guillermo Kuitca*, Centro de Arte Reina Sofía, Palacio de Velázquez, Madrid, and the Museo de Arte Latinoamericano de Buenos Aires (2003); *Lucio Fontana*, Centro Cultural do Banco do Brasil, Rio de Janeiro and São Paulo (2001); and *The Trajectory of Light in Brazilian Art*, Instituto Cultural Itaú, São Paulo (2001). His publications include *Vik Muniz* (Aprazível Edições, 2009), *Louise Bourgeois* (Rizzoli, 2008), *Seu Sami – Hilal Sami Hilal* (Museu Vale do Rio Doce, 2007), *Rebecca Horn: Body Landscapes* (Hatje Cantz, 2005), *Jorge de la Vega: Obras 1961–1971* (Museo de Arte Latinoamericano de Buenos Aires, 2004), *How Latitudes Become Forms: Art in a Global Age* (Walker Art Center, 2003), and *Tempo* (Museum of Modern Art, New York, 2002), among many others.

Carrie Lambert-Beatty

Carrie Lambert-Beatty is Assistant Professor of Visual and Environmental Studies and of History of Art and Architecture at Harvard University. Her research focuses on art since 1960, especially performance and video. She received her Ph.D. from Stanford University in 2002. She has been a fellow at the Whitney Museum of American Art Independent Study Program and the Getty Research Institute. Her writing on performance art, postmodern dance, and minimalism has been published in exhibition catalogues and journals such as *Trans*, *Art Journal*, and *October*, of which she has been an editor since 2008. Her book *Being Watched: Yvonne Rainer and the 1960s* (MIT Press, 2008) was the 2008 winner of the de la Torre prize for scholarship on dance. Lambert-Beatty is working on a new project on recent intersections of art and activism, parts of which have been published in the journal *Signs* (Winter 2008) and *October* (Summer 2009).

Gabriela Rangel

Gabriela Rangel holds an M.A. in curatorial studies from the Center for Curatorial Studies at Bard College, an M.A. in media and communications studies from the Universidad Católica Andrés Bello in Caracas, and a B.A. in film studies from the International Film School at San Antonio de los Baños, Cuba. She is currently the Director of Visual Arts at Americas Society. Prior to this position she was Assistant Curator of Latin American art and Programs Coordinator for the International Center for the Arts of the Americas at the Museum of Fine Arts, Houston. She has curated exhibitions dedicated to Gordon Matta-Clark, Carlos Cruz-Diez, Juan Downey, and Dias & Riedweg, among many others. Rangel's publications include contributions to the catalogues *Arturo Herrera* (Trasnocho Arte Contacto, 2009), *Arte no es vida* (El Museo del Barrio, 2008), *A Principality of Its Own* (Americas Society, 2006), *Liliana Porter* (Centro de Arte Recoleta de Buenos Aires, 2003), and *Da Adversidade Vivemos: Artistes d'Amérique latine* (Musée d'Art Moderne de la Ville de Paris, 2001), among others.

Lane Relyea

Lane Relyea is Associate Professor of Art Theory and Practice at North-western University. His essays and reviews have appeared in numerous magazines, including *Artforum, Parkett, Frieze, Art in America, After*, and *Flash Art*. He has written monographs on Polly Apfelbaum (MassArt, 2004); Richard Artschwager (Gagosian Gallery, 2002); Jeremy Blake (Blaffer Gallery, University of Houston, 2002); Vija Celmins (Phaidon Press, 2004); Toba Khedoori (Offentliche Kunstsammlung, 2001); Monique Prieto (ACME and Corvi-Mora Gallery, 2002); and Wolfgang Tillmans (Museum of Contemporary Art, Chicago, and Hammer Museum, 2006). He has contributed to several exhibition catalogues, including *Public Offerings* and *Helter Skelter* (both Museum of Contemporary Art, Los Angeles, 2001 and 1992 respectively), and his writings have appeared in numerous journals and publications, including *X-tra, Afterall*, and *Critical Mess: Art Critics on the State of their Practice,* edited by Raphael Rubinstein (Hard Press Editions, 2006).

Nicolau Sevcenko

Nicolau Sevcenko is Professor of Romance Languages and Literatures at Harvard University, where his research focuses on modern Brazilian culture, particularly the relationship between society and culture; twentieth-century Brazil; and modernity and postmodernity. He is on the faculty of the University of São Paulo and has published widely on Brazilian history, literature, and culture. His titles include *Literatura como Missão: Tensões Sociais e Criação Cultural na Primeira República* (Companhia das Letras, 2003), *Pindorama Revisitada: Cultura e Sociedade em Tempos de Virada* (Fundação Peirópolis, 2000); and *Orfeu Extático na Metrópole: São Paulo, Sociedade e Cultura nos Frementes Anos 20* (Companhia das Letras, 1992).

Doris Sommer

Doris Sommer is Ira Jewell Williams, Jr., Professor of Romance Languages and Literatures and in African and African American Studies at Harvard University. She received a B.A. in English Literature at Hebrew University of Jerusalem, and a B.A., *cum laude,* in Spanish Language and Literature at Rutgers University. She completed a Masters in Comparative Literature at Rutgers University, and in Hispanic Literature at the Hebrew University of Jerusalem. She received her Ph.D. in Comparative Literature at Rutgers University in 1977. At Harvard, she is Director of the Cultural Agents Initiative. She has received numerous grants, including a John Simon Guggenheim Foundation Fellowship in 1995. She has published several books, including *Bilingual Games: Some Literary Inventions* (Palgrave-Macmillan, 2002) and *Bilingual Aesthetics: A New Sentimental Education* (Duke University Press, 2004), as well as numerous articles.

SELECTED BIBLIOGRAPHY

Ashford, Doug. "The Exhibition as an Artistic Medium." *Art Journal* 57, no. 2 (Summer 1998), pp. 28–37.

Benjamin, Walter. *Reflections: Essays, Aphorisms, Autobiographical Writings,* edited and with an introduction by Peter Demetz. New York: Schocken Books, 1986. First published 1978 by Harcourt Brace Jovanovich.

Bishop, Claire. "Antagonism and Relational Aesthetics." *October* 110 (Autumn 2004), pp. 51–79.

———, ed. *Participation (Documents of Contemporary Art).* Cambridge, MA and London: The MIT Press, 2006.

———. "The Social Turn: Collaboration and Its Discontents." *Artforum* 44, no. 6 (February 2006), pp. 178–83.

Blazwick, Iwona, Susan Cahan, Andrea Fraser, Michael Clegg, Martin Guttmann, Ute Meta Bauer, and Stephan Dillemuth. "Serving Audiences." *October* 80 (Spring 1997), pp. 128–39.

Bourriaud, Nicolas. *Relational Aesthetics*, trans. Simon Pleasance and Fronza Woods with the participation of Mathieu Copeland. [Dijon]: Les Presses du réel, 2002. Originally published as *Esthétique relationnelle* ([Dijon]: Les Presses du réel, 1997).

Cameron, Dan. "'80s Then: Group Material Talks to Dan Cameron." *Artforum* 41, no. 8 (April 2003), pp. 198–99.

Crimp, Douglas, Rosalyn Deutsche, Ewa Lajer-Burcharth, and Krzysztof Wodiczko. "A Conversation with Krzysztof Wodiczko." *October* 37 (Autumn 1986), pp. 23–51.

Critical Art Ensemble. "Observations on Collective Cultural Action." *Art Journal* 57, no. 2 (Summer 1998), pp. 72–85.

Foster, Hal. *The Return of the Real: The Avant-Garde at the End of the Century,* especially "The Artist as Ethnographer," pp. 171–203. Cambridge, MA and London: The MIT Press, 1996.

Foucault, Michel. "What Is an Author?" In *The Foucault Reader*, edited by Paul Rabinow, pp. 101–20. New York: Pantheon, 1984.

Gablik, Suzi. "Connective Aesthetics." *American Art* 6, no. 2 (Spring 1992), pp. 2–7.

Gillick, Liam. "Letters and Responses." *October* 115 (Winter 2006), pp. 95–106.

Goldbard, Arlene. "When (Art) Worlds Collide: Institutionalizing Alternatives." In *Alternative Art New York, 1965–1985,* edited by Julie Ault, pp. 183–200. Minneapolis: University of Minnesota Press, 2003.

Group Material. "A Project by Group Material." *Art Journal* 50, no. 3 (Autumn 1991), pp. 38–39.

Habermas, Jürgen. *The Philosophical Discourse of Modernity,* trans. Frederick Lawrence. Cambridge, MA and London: The MIT Press, 1987.

Kester, Grant H. *Conversation Pieces: Community and Communication in Modern Art*, especially "Dialogical Aesthetics," pp. 82–123. Berkeley: University of California Press, 2004.

Kwon, Mikwon. *One Place After Another: Site-Specific Art and Locational Identity.* Cambridge, MA and London: The MIT Press, 2002.

McDonough, Tom. "City of Cineastes." *Art in America* 94, no. 8 (September 2006), pp. 60–64.

Mouffe, Chantal. *On the Political.* New York: Routledge, 2005.

Placky, Robert. "On Site: A Residency with Tim Rollins/KOS." *Art Education* 53, no. 4 (July 2000), pp. 50–54.

Rangel, Gabriela. "*Paula Trope and the 'Meninos do Morrinho,'*" trans. Clifford Landers. *Review: Literature and Arts of the Americas* 39, no. 2 (2006), pp. 277–83.

Relyea, Lane. "Your Art World: Or, The Limits of Connectivity." *Afterall* 14 (Autumn/Winter 2006), pp. 3–8.

Roche, Jennifer. "Socially Engaged Art, Critics and Discontents: An Interview with Claire Bishop." *Community Arts Network: Reading Room* (July 2006). http://www.communityarts.net/readingroom.

Weintraub, Linda. *In the Making: Creative Options for Contemporary Art History Classes.* New York: Distributed Arts Publishers, 2003.

Willett, John, ed. and trans. *Brecht on Theatre: The Development of an Aesthetic.* New York: Hill and Wang, 1964.